Practical Cloud Native Security with Falco

Risk and Threat Detection for Containers, Kubernetes, and Cloud

Loris Degioanni and Leonardo Grasso

Beijing · Boston · Farnham · Sebastopol · Tokyo

Practical Cloud Native Security with Falco

by Loris Degioanni and Leonardo Grasso

Published by O'Reilly Media, Inc., 1005 Gravenstein Highway North, Sebastopol, CA 95472.

O'Reilly books may be purchased for educational, business, or sales promotional use. Online editions are also available for most titles (*http://oreilly.com*). For more information, contact our corporate/institutional sales department: 800-998-9938 or *corporate@oreilly.com*.

Acquisitions Editor: Jennifer Pollock	**Indexer:** WordCo Indexing Services, Inc.
Development Editor: Sarah Grey	**Interior Designer:** David Futato
Production Editor: Gregory Hyman	**Cover Designer:** Karen Montgomery
Copyeditor: Rachel Head	**Illustrator:** Kate Dullea
Proofreader: Kim Wimpsett	

August 2022:   First Edition

Revision History for the First Edition

2022-08-10:   First Release

See *http://oreilly.com/catalog/errata.csp?isbn=9781098118570* for release details.

978-1-098-11857-0

[LSI]

Table of Contents

Preface

The advent of modern computing stacks is radically changing how we think about security. In the old data center days, security practitioners thought of software applications as medieval castles: securing them involved building big walls with small, well-guarded openings. Modern cloud-based software looks more like a bustling modern city: people move freely inside it and across its limits to consume and provide services and buy, sell, build, and fix things.

As today's urban planners know, big walls and guarded entrances alone are not enough to secure a city. A better approach involves widespread, granular visibility: a network of security cameras, for example, plus the ability to view their footage and react to any threats they capture in real time.

This book is about security for modern applications, using the open source tool that the industry has embraced as the "security camera" for the cloud native stack: Falco. Falco is a cloud native runtime security project designed to protect software that runs in the cloud by detecting unexpected behavior, intrusions, and data theft in real time. It's the de facto threat detection engine for Kubernetes and for cloud infrastructure, deployed by countless users, from single-machine test environments to some of the biggest computing environments on the planet. We'll teach you how you can protect applications as they run by detecting threats and misconfigurations in workloads and in the cloud infrastructure where they operate.

We have a very practical goal in this book: giving you the knowledge you need to successfully deploy runtime security in your environment, regardless of its scale, using Falco. By the time you've finished reading the book, you will have a solid understanding of how Falco works: you'll be able to install it in any environment, tune its performance, customize it for your needs, collect and interpret its data, and even extend it.

Who Is This Book For?

We wrote this book primarily for security operators and architects who want to implement runtime security and threat detection in production in their modern computing environments. However, we've designed it to be approachable even for readers with limited or no experience in the field. For that reason, we only require that you have familiarity with the most important cloud computing services, with containers, and with Kubernetes.

We'll also cover more advanced topics like deployment at scale, optimization, and rule writing that even expert users will find useful. So, even if you are familiar with runtime security, and perhaps are already using Falco, this book will help you step up your game. The latter part of the book requires basic knowledge of programming languages like Go. Developers who want to extend or customize Falco will find much value here. Finally, we've geared the last chapter of the book toward those who are considering becoming Falco contributors—we hope we'll inspire you to join them!

Overview

The book is divided into four parts, organized in order of increasing complexity, with each successive part building on the previous one. To help you get oriented, let's take a look at the content of each part.

Part I: The Basics

Part I is about what Falco is and does. Here, we will teach you the fundamental concepts behind Falco and guide you through your first local deployment:

- Chapter 1, "Introducing Falco", gives an overview of what Falco is, including a high-level view of its functionality and an introductory description of each of its components. The chapter includes a brief history of Falco and a look at the tools that inspired it.

- Chapter 2, "Getting Started with Falco on Your Local Machine", guides you through the process of installing a single Falco instance on your local Linux box. The chapter includes instructions on how to run Falco and generate your first notification output.

Part II: The Architecture of Falco

Part II will teach you about the intricacies of Falco's architecture and inner workings:

- Chapter 3, "Understanding Falco's Architecture", dives into the details of Falco sensors, how data collection happens, and what components are involved in processing it. The architectural understanding you will gain from this chapter is the base for the rest of the book.

- Chapter 4, "Data Sources", is about understanding the two main data sources you can use in Falco: system calls and plugins. We explain what the data produced by these sources is, how it is collected, and how Falco's collection stack compares with alternative approaches.

- Chapter 5, "Data Enrichment", covers techniques Falco uses to enrich the data it collects. Enrichment consists of adding layers of contextual information to the collected data; for example, container IDs, Kubernetes labels, or cloud provider tags. This chapter explains how to configure Falco to collect enrichment metadata and how to customize it to add your own metadata.

- Chapter 6, "Fields and Filters", covers one of the most important concepts in Falco—the filtering engine—and the fields at its base. The chapter is structured as a reference for the language syntax (including operators) and the fields.

- Chapter 7, "Falco Rules", introduces rules and their syntax, including constructs like lists and macros that you will use routinely when customizing Falco.

- Chapter 8, "The Output Framework", describes the mechanism Falco uses to deliver notifications to output channels and the channels available in Falco, and teaches you how to configure and use them.

Part III: Running Falco in Production

Part III is the reference manual for the serious Falco user. This part of the book will teach you everything you need to know to deploy, configure, run, and tune Falco in any environment:

- Chapter 9, "Installing Falco", presents approaches to installing Falco in production environments, with detailed instructions.

- Chapter 10, "Configuring and Running Falco", covers how Falco's configuration system works. This chapter will help you understand and use Falco settings, including command-line options, environment variables, the configuration file, and rules files.

- Chapter 11, "Using Falco for Cloud Security", offers a general overview of cloud security, then goes into the specifics of AWS threat detection using Falco's CloudTrail plugin. It takes a practical approach and includes clear and complete instructions for setting up cloud security in your environment using Falco.

- Chapter 12, "Consuming Falco Events", focuses on what you can do with Falco's detections. It covers tools that help you work with Falco outputs, like falco-explorer and Falcosidekick, and helps you understand which Falco events are useful to observe and analyze as well as how to process them.

Part IV: Extending Falco

Part IV is a reference for developers, covering methods for extending Falco:

- Chapter 13, "Writing Falco Rules", is about customizing and extending Falco's detections. You will learn how to write new rules and tune existing rules for your needs. In addition to the basics of rule writing, the chapter covers advanced topics like noise reduction, performance optimization, and tagging.
- Chapter 14, "Falco Development", is about working with Falco's source code. It begins with an overview of the code base, then dives into two important ways of extending Falco: using the gRPC API and the plugins framework. You will find several examples that you can use as the basis for your coding adventures.
- Chapter 15, "How to Contribute", talks about the Falco community and shows you how to contribute to it. It's ideal reading if, after staying with us for the whole book, you are as excited as we are about Falco!

Conventions Used in This Book

The following typographical conventions are used in this book:

Italic
: Indicates new terms, URLs, email addresses, filenames, and file extensions.

`Constant width`
: Used for command-line input and program listings, as well as within paragraphs to refer to commands and program elements such as variable or function names, data types, and environment variables.

`Constant width bold`
: Shows commands or other text that should be typed literally by the user. Also used occasionally in program listings to highlight text of interest.

`Constant width italic`
: Shows text that should be replaced with user-supplied values or by values determined by context.

 This element signifies a tip or suggestion.

This element signifies a general note.

 This element indicates a warning or caution.

Using Code Examples

Code examples from Chapter 14 are available for download at *https://oreil.ly/practical-cloud-native-security-falco-code*.

If you have a technical question or a problem using the code examples, please send email to *bookquestions@oreilly.com*.

This book is here to help you get your job done. In general, if example code is offered with this book, you may use it in your programs and documentation. You do not need to contact us for permission unless you're reproducing a significant portion of the code. For example, writing a program that uses several chunks of code from this book does not require permission. Selling or distributing a CD-ROM of examples from O'Reilly books does require permission. Answering a question by citing this book and quoting example code does not require permission. Incorporating a significant amount of example code from this book into your product's documentation does require permission.

We appreciate, but do not require, attribution. An attribution usually includes the title, author, publisher, and ISBN. For example: "*Practical Cloud Native Security with Falco*, by Loris Degioanni and Leonardo Grasso (O'Reilly). Copyright 2022 O'Reilly Media, Inc., 978-1-098-11857-0."

If you feel your use of code examples falls outside fair use or the permission given above, feel free to contact us at *permissions@oreilly.com*.

O'Reilly Online Learning

For more than 40 years, O'Reilly Media has provided technology and business training, knowledge, and insight to help companies succeed.

Our unique network of experts and innovators share their knowledge and expertise through books, articles, and our online learning platform. O'Reilly's online learning platform gives you on-demand access to live training courses, in-depth learning paths, interactive coding environments, and a vast collection of text and video from O'Reilly and 200+ other publishers. For more information, visit *http://oreilly.com*.

How to Contact Us

Please address comments and questions concerning this book to the publisher:

> O'Reilly Media, Inc.
> 1005 Gravenstein Highway North
> Sebastopol, CA 95472
> 800-998-9938 (in the United States or Canada)
> 707-829-0515 (international or local)
> 707-829-0104 (fax)

We have a web page for this book, where we list errata, examples, and any additional information. You can access this page at *https://oreil.ly/practical-cloud-native-security-falco*.

Email *bookquestions@oreilly.com* to comment or ask technical questions about this book.

For news and information about our books and courses, visit *https://oreilly.com*.

Find us on LinkedIn: *https://linkedin.com/company/oreilly-media*

Follow us on Twitter: *https://twitter.com/oreillymedia*

Watch us on YouTube: *https://www.youtube.com/oreillymedia*

Acknowledgments

We would like to start by thanking, from the bottom of our hearts, the Falco community: the maintainers who spend countless hours running and growing the project with incredible passion; the contributors, big and small, who make Falco better every day; the adopters and champions who give Falco a chance and provide valuable feedback. Falco, clearly, is the product of your love and talent, and it will be an honor for us if this book can showcase your incredible work.

Thanks also to the Cloud Native Computing Foundation, for providing a good home for Falco and supporting its growth.

We would like to thank as well the people who helped us and supported us while writing this book: in particular, our project manager, Tammy Yue, and our O'Reilly editor, Sarah Grey. You have been not only very professional and helpful, but also extremely gracious, constructive, and patient. Working with you has been a true pleasure.

Finally, this book would not have been possible without the support of Sysdig, the company where we both work. We truly appreciate working for an organization that not only understands but actively supports open source and that embraces our belief that the future of security is open.

Leonardo

One day, while I was talking to Loris, he proposed that we should write a book together. So as I'm here, I have to thank him first. Working on this idea with him was one of the most challenging but, at the same time, fun things I've done in my life. Shall we do it again? As a first-time author, writing this book has been an incredible new adventure for me that wouldn't have been possible without the help and love of my family. So, I would like to thank my shining and beloved Ada, who has always supported me and has given me our little Michelangelo. I also want to thank our little boy for waiting in his mommy's belly until right after his daddy completed writing this book. Together with Ma~ (read "Matilde," our little kitten who purred next to me while I was writing), they have accompanied me with patience and joy during this journey.

Last but not least, I also have to thank my parents, sister, and uncles with all my heart. They have always believed in me, sustained me, and helped me whenever needed. I couldn't make it through without them, seriously.

Loris

I would like to thank my wife Stacey, the love of my life, for her patience and undeterred support for what I do. Thank you for not letting me starve, drown, or generally injure myself during the production of this book.

I also want to thank my three kids, Josephine, Vincenzo, and August, for bringing happiness to every minute of my life, including the time spent working on this publication. Your frequent questions and interruptions made writing this book more challenging but also much more pleasant. I'm looking forward to reading the books that you will publish when you grow up.

I would like to thank my parents for supporting me at (and before) the beginning of my career. I wouldn't be writing this preface today without the seeds that you planted many years ago and watered with love and generosity.

This book would have not been possible without my coauthor, Leo. The two of us had to spend a *lot* of time together to produce this work, and every minute with him was pleasant, constructive, and fun. Leo, I'm looking forward to spending time with you on more fun and ambitious projects in the future.

PART I

The Basics

CHAPTER 1

Introducing Falco

The goal of this first chapter of the book is to explain what Falco is. Don't worry, we'll take it easy! We will first look at what Falco does, including a high-level view of its functionality and an introductory description of each of its components. We'll explore the design principles that inspired Falco and still guide its development today. We'll then discuss what you can do with Falco, what is outside its domain, and what you can better accomplish with other tools. Finally, we'll provide some historical context to put things into perspective.

Falco in a Nutshell

At the highest level, Falco is pretty straightforward: you deploy it by installing multiple *sensors* across a distributed infrastructure. Each sensor collects data (from the local machine or by talking to some API), runs a set of rules against it, and notifies you if something bad happens. Figure 1-1 shows a simplified diagram of how it works.

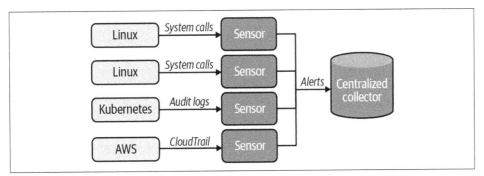

Figure 1-1. Falco's high-level architecture

You can think of Falco like a network of security cameras for your infrastructure: you place the sensors in key locations, they observe what's going on, and they ping you if they detect harmful behavior. With Falco, bad behavior is defined by a set of rules that the community created and maintains for you and that you can customize or extend for your needs. The alerts generated by your fleet of Falco sensors can theoretically stay in the local machine, but in practice they are typically exported to a centralized collector. For centralized alert collection, you can use a general-purpose security information and event management (SIEM) tool or a specialized tool like Falcosidekick. (We'll cover alert collection extensively in Chapter 12.)

Now let's dig a little deeper into the Falco architecture and explore its main components, starting with the sensors.

Sensors

Figure 1-2 shows how Falco sensors work.

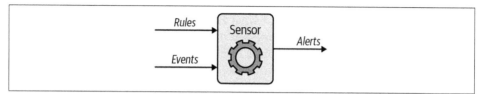

Figure 1-2. Falco sensor architecture

The sensor consists of an engine that has two inputs: a data source and a set of rules. The sensor applies the rules to each event coming from the data source. When a rule matches an event, an output message is produced. Very straightforward, right?

Data Sources

Each sensor is able to collect input data from a number of sources. Originally, Falco was designed to exclusively operate on system calls, which to date remain one of its most important data sources. We'll cover system calls in detail in Chapters 3 and 4, but for now you can think of them as what a running program uses to interface with its external world. Opening or closing a file, establishing or receiving a network connection, reading and writing data to and from the disk or the network, executing commands, and communicating with other processes using pipes or other types of interprocess communication are all examples of system call usage.

Falco collects system calls by instrumenting the kernel of the Linux operating system (OS). It can do this in two different ways: deploying a kernel module (i.e., a piece of executable code that can be installed in the operating system kernel to extend the kernel's functionality) or using a technology called eBPF, which allows running of scripts that safely perform actions inside the OS. We'll talk extensively about kernel modules and eBPF in Chapter 4.

Tapping into this data gives Falco incredible visibility into everything that is happening in your infrastructure. Here are some examples of things Falco can detect for you:

- Privilege escalations
- Access to sensitive data
- Ownership and mode changes
- Unexpected network connections or socket mutations
- Unwanted program execution
- Data exfiltration
- Compliance violations

Falco has also been extended to tap into other data sources besides system calls (we'll show you examples throughout the book). For example, Falco can monitor your cloud logs in real time and notify you when something bad happens in your cloud infrastructure. Here are some more examples of things it can detect for you:

- When a user logs in without multifactor authentication
- When a cloud service configuration is modified
- When somebody accesses one or more sensitive files in an Amazon Web Services (AWS) S3 bucket

New data sources are added to Falco frequently, so we recommend checking the website (*https://falco.org*) and Slack channel (*https://oreil.ly/Y4bUt*) to keep up with what's new.

Rules

Rules tell the Falco engine what to do with the data coming from the sources. They allow the user to define policies in a compact and readable format. Falco comes preloaded with a comprehensive set of rules that cover host, container, Kubernetes, and cloud security, and you can easily create your own rules to customize it. We'll spend a lot of time on rules, in particular in Chapters 7 and 13; by the time you're done reading this book, you'll be a total master at them. Here's an example to whet your appetite:

```
- rule: shell_in_container
  desc: shell opened inside a container
  condition: spawned_process and container.id != host and proc.name = bash
  output: shell in a container (user=%user.name container_id=%container.id)
```

```
Source: syscall
priority: WARNING
```

This rule detects when a bash shell is started inside a container, which is normally not a good thing in an immutable container-based infrastructure. The core entries in a rule are the *condition*, which tells Falco what to look at, and the *output*, which is what Falco will tell you when the condition triggers. As you can see, both the condition and the output act on *fields*, one of the core concepts in Falco. The condition is a Boolean expression that combines checks of fields against values (essentially, a filter). The output is a combination of text and field names, whose values will be printed out in the notification. Its syntax is similar to that of a `print` statement in a programming language.

Does this remind you of networking tools like tcpdump or Wireshark? Good eye: they were a big inspiration for Falco.

Data Enrichment

Rich data sources and a flexible rule engine help make Falco a powerful runtime security tool. On top of that, metadata from a disparate set of providers enriches its detections.

When Falco tells you that something has happened—for example, that a system file has been modified—you typically need more information to understand the cause and the scope of the issue. Which process did this? Did it happen in a container? If so, what were the container and image names? What was the service/namespace where this happened? Was it in production or in dev? Was this a change made by root?

Falco's data enrichment engine helps answer all of these questions by building up the environment state, including running processes and threads, the files they have open, the containers and Kubernetes objects they run in, etc. All of this state is accessible to Falco's rules and outputs. For example, you can easily scope a rule so that it triggers only in production or in a specific service.

Output Channels

Every time a rule is triggered, the corresponding engine emits an output notification. In the simplest possible configuration, the engine writes the notification to standard output (which, as you can imagine, usually isn't very useful). Fortunately, Falco offers sophisticated ways to route outputs and direct them to a bunch of places, including log collection tools, cloud storage services like S3, and communication tools like Slack and email. Its ecosystem includes a fantastic project called Falcosidekick, specifically designed to connect Falco to the world and make output collection effortless (see Chapter 12 for more on this).

Containers and More

Falco was designed for the modern world of cloud native applications, so it has excellent out-of-the-box support for containers, Kubernetes, and the cloud. Since this book is about cloud native security, we will mostly focus on that, but keep in mind that Falco is not limited to containers and Kubernetes running in the cloud. You can absolutely use it as a host security tool, and many of its preloaded rules can help you secure your fleet of Linux servers. Falco also has good support for network detection, allowing you to inspect the activity of connections, IP addresses, ports, clients, and servers and receive alerts when they show unwanted or unexpected/atypical behavior.

Falco's Design Principles

Now that you understand what Falco does, let's talk about why it is the way it is. When you're developing a piece of software of non-negligible complexity, it's important to focus on the right use cases and prioritize the most important goals. Sometimes that means accepting trade-offs. Falco is no exception. Its development has been guided by a core set of principles. In this section we will explore why they were chosen and how each of them affects Falco's architecture and feature set. Understanding these principles will allow you to judge whether Falco is a good fit for your use cases and help you get the most out of it.

Specialized for Runtime

The Falco engine is designed to detect threats while your services and applications are running. When it detects unwanted behavior, Falco should alert you instantly (at most in a matter of seconds) so you're informed (and can react!) right away, not after minutes or hours have passed.

This design principle manifests in three important architectural choices. First, the Falco engine is engineered as a streaming engine, able to process data quickly as it arrives rather than storing it and acting on it later. Second, it's designed to evaluate each event independently, not to generate alerts based on a sequence of events; this means correlating different events, even if feasible, is not a primary goal and is in fact discouraged. Third, Falco evaluates rules as close as possible to the data source. If possible, it avoids transporting information before processing it and favors deploying richer engines on the endpoints.

Suitable for Production

You should be able to deploy Falco in any environment, including production environments where stability and low overhead are of paramount importance. It should not crash your apps and should strive to slow them down as little as possible.

This design principle affects the data collection architecture, particularly when Falco runs on endpoints that have many processes or containers. Falco's drivers (the kernel module and eBPF probe) have undergone many iterations and years of testing to guarantee their performance and stability. Collecting data by tapping into the kernel of the operating system, as opposed to instrumenting the monitored processes/containers, guarantees that your applications won't crash because of bugs in Falco.

The Falco engine is written in C++ and employs many expedients to reduce resource consumption. For example, it avoids processing system calls that read or write disk or network data. In some ways this is a limitation, because it prevents users from creating rules that inspect the content of payloads, but it also ensures that CPU and memory consumption stay low, which is more important.

Intent-Free Instrumentation

Falco is designed to observe application behavior without requiring users to recompile applications, install libraries, or rebuild containers with monitoring hooks. This is very important in modern containerized environments, where applying changes to every component would require an unrealistic amount of work. It also guarantees that Falco sees every process and container, no matter where it comes from, who runs it, or how long it's been around.

Optimized to Run at the Edge

Compared to other policy engines (for example, OPA), Falco has been explicitly designed with a distributed, multisensor architecture in mind. Its sensors are designed to be lightweight, efficient, and portable, and to operate in diverse environments. It can be deployed on a physical host, in a virtual machine, or as a container. The Falco binary is built for multiple platforms, including ARM.

Avoids Moving and Storing a Ton of Data

Most currently marketed threat detection products are based on sending large numbers of events to a centralized SIEM tool and then performing analytics on top of the collected data. Falco is designed around a very different principle: stay as close as possible to the endpoint, perform detections in place, and only ship alerts to a centralized collector. This approach results in a solution that is a bit less capable at performing complex analytics, but is simple to operate, much more cost-effective, and scales very well horizontally.

Scalable

Speaking of scale, another important design goal underlying Falco is that it should be able to scale to support the biggest infrastructures in the world. If you can run it,

Falco should be able to secure it. As we've just described, keeping limited state and avoiding centralized storage are important elements of this. Edge computing is an important element too, since distributing rule evaluation is the only approach to scale a tool like Falco in a truly horizontal way.

Another key part of scalability is endpoint instrumentation. Falco's data collection stack doesn't use techniques like sidecars, library linking, or process instrumentation. The reason is that the resource utilization of all of these techniques grows with the number of containers, libraries, or processes to monitor. Busy machines have many containers, libraries, and processes—too many for these techniques to work—but they have only one operating system kernel. Capturing system calls in the kernel means that you need only one Falco sensor per machine, no matter how big the machine is. This makes it possible to run Falco on big hosts with a lot of activity.

Truthful

One other benefit of using system calls as a data source? System calls never lie. Falco is hard to evade because the mechanism it uses to collect data is very difficult to disable or circumvent. If you try to evade or get around it, you will leave traces that Falco can capture.

Robust Defaults, Richly Extensible

Another key design goal was minimizing the time it takes to extract value from Falco. You should be able to do this by just installing it; you shouldn't need to customize it unless you have advanced requirements.

Whenever the need for customization does arise, though, Falco offers flexibility. For example, you can create new rules through a rich and expressive syntax, develop and deploy new data sources that expand the scope of detections, and integrate Falco with your desired notification and event collection tools.

Simple

Simplicity is the last design choice underpinning Falco, but it's also one of the most important ones. The Falco rule syntax is designed to be compact, easy to read, and simple to learn. Whenever possible, a Falco rule condition should fit in a single line. Anyone, not only experts, should be able to write a new rule or modify an existing one. It's OK if this reduces the expressiveness of the syntax: Falco is in the business of delivering an efficient security rule engine, not a full-fledged domain-specific language. There are better tools for that.

Simplicity is also evident in the processes for extending Falco to alert on new data sources and integrating it with a new cloud service or type of container, which is a matter of writing a plugin in any language, including Go, C, and C++. Falco loads these plugins easily, and you can use them to add support for new data sources or new fields to use in rules.

What You Can Do with Falco

Falco shines at detecting threats, intrusions, and data theft at runtime and in real time. It works well with legacy infrastructures but excels at supporting containers, Kubernetes, and cloud infrastructures. It secures both workloads (processes, containers, services) and infrastructure (hosts, VMs, network, cloud infrastructure and services). It is designed to be lightweight, efficient, and scalable and to be used in both development and production. It can detect many classes of threats, but should you need more, you can customize it. It also has a thriving community that supports it and keeps enhancing it.

What You Cannot Do with Falco

No single tool can solve all your problems. Knowing what you cannot do with Falco is as important as knowing where to use it. As with any tool, there are trade-offs. First, Falco is not a general-purpose policy language: it doesn't offer the expressiveness of a full programming language and cannot perform correlation across different engines. Its rule engine, instead, is designed to apply relatively stateless rules at high frequency in many places around your infrastructure. If you are looking for a powerful centralized policy language, we suggest you take a look at OPA (*https://oreil.ly/nXYQI*).

Second, Falco is not designed to store the data it collects in a centralized repository so that you can perform analytics on it. Rule validation is performed at the endpoint, and only the alerts are sent to a centralized location. If your focus is advanced analytics and big data querying, we recommend that you use one of the many log collection tools available on the market.

Finally, for efficiency reasons, Falco does not inspect network payloads. Therefore, it's not the right tool to implement layer 7 (L7) security policies. A traditional network-based intrusion detection system (IDS) or L7 firewall is a better choice for such a use case.

Background and History

The authors of this book have been part of some of Falco's history, and this final section presents our memories and perspectives. If you are interested only in operationalizing Falco, feel free to skip the rest of this chapter. However, we believe that knowing where Falco comes from can give you useful context for its architecture that will ultimately help you use it better. Plus, it's a fun story!

Network Packets: BPF, libpcap, tcpdump, and Wireshark

During the height of the late-1990s internet boom, computer networks were exploding in popularity. So was the need to observe, troubleshoot, and secure them. Unfortunately, many operators couldn't afford the network visibility tools available at that time, which were all commercially offered and very expensive. As a consequence, a lot of people were fumbling around in the dark.

Soon, teams around the world started working on solutions to this problem. Some involved extending existing operating systems to add packet capture functionality: in other words, making it possible to convert an off-the-shelf computer workstation into a device that could sit on a network and collect all the packets sent or received by other workstations. One such solution, Berkeley Packet Filter (BPF), developed by Steven McCanne and Van Jacobson at the University of California at Berkeley, was designed to extend the BSD operating system kernel. If you use Linux, you might be familiar with eBPF, a virtual machine that can be used to safely execute arbitrary code in the Linux kernel (the *e* stands for *extended*). eBPF is one of the hottest modern features of the Linux kernel. It's evolved into an extremely powerful and flexible technology after many years of improvements, but it started as a little programmable packet capture and filtering module for BSD Unix.

BPF came with a library called *libpcap* that any program could use to capture raw network packets. Its availability triggered a proliferation of networking and security tools. The first tool based on *libpcap* was a command-line network analyzer called tcpdump, which is still part of virtually any Unix distribution. In 1998, however, a GUI-based open source protocol analyzer called Ethereal (renamed Wireshark in 2006) was launched. It became, and still is, the industry standard for packet analysis.

What tcpdump, Wireshark, and many other popular networking tools have in common is the ability to access a data source that is rich, accurate, and trustworthy and can be collected in a noninvasive way: raw network packets. Keep this concept in mind as you continue reading!

Snort and Packet-Based Runtime Security

Introspection tools like tcpdump and Wireshark were the natural early applications of the BPF packet capture stack. However, people soon started getting creative in their use cases for packets. For example, in 1998, Martin Roesch released an open source network intrusion detection tool called Snort. Snort is a rule engine that processes packets captured from the network. It has a large set of rules that can detect threats and unwanted activity by looking at packets, the protocols they contain, and the payloads they carry. It inspired the creation of similar tools such as Suricata and Zeek.

What makes tools like Snort powerful is their ability to validate the security of networks and applications *while applications are running*. This is important because it provides real-time protection, and the focus on runtime behavior makes it possible to detect threats based on vulnerabilities that have not yet been disclosed.

The Network Packets Crisis

You've just seen what made network packets popular as a data source for visibility, security, and troubleshooting. Applications based on them spawned several successful industries. However, trends arose that eroded packets' usefulness as a source of truth:

- Collecting packets in a comprehensive way became more and more complicated, especially in environments like the cloud, where access to routers and network infrastructure is limited.

- Encryption and network virtualization made it more challenging to extract valuable information.

- The rise of containers and orchestrators like Kubernetes made infrastructures more elastic. At the same time, it became more complicated to reliably collect network data.

These issues started becoming clear in the early 2010s, with the popularity of cloud computing and containers. Once again, an exciting new ecosystem was unfolding, but no one quite knew how to troubleshoot and secure it.

System Calls as a Data Source: sysdig

That's where your authors come in. We released an open source tool called *sysdig*, which we were inspired to build by a set of questions: What is the best way to provide visibility for modern cloud native applications? Can we apply workflows built on top of packet capture to this new world? What is the best data source?

sysdig originally focused on collecting system calls from the kernel of the operating system. System calls are a rich data source—even richer than packets—because they don't exclusively focus on network data: they include file I/O, command execution, interprocess communication, and more. They are a better data source for cloud native environments than packets, because they can be collected from the kernel for both containers and cloud instances. Plus, collecting them is easy, efficient, and minimally invasive.

sysdig was initially composed of three separate components:

- A kernel capture probe (available in two flavors, kernel module and eBPF)
- A set of libraries to facilitate the development of capture programs
- A command-line tool with decoding and filtering capabilities

In other words, it was porting the BPF stack to system calls. sysdig was engineered to support the most popular network packet workflows: trace files, easy filtering, scriptability, and so on. From the beginning, we also included native integrations with Kubernetes and other orchestrators, with the goal of making them useful in modern environments. sysdig immediately became very popular with the community, validating the technical approach.

Falco

So what would be the next logical step? You guessed it: a Snort-like tool for system calls! A flexible rule engine on top of the sysdig libraries, we thought, would be a powerful tool to detect anomalous behavior and intrusions in modern apps reliably and efficiently—essentially the Snort approach but applied to system calls and designed to work in the cloud.

So, that's how Falco was born. The first (rather simple) version was released at the end of 2016 and included most of the important components, such as the rule engine. Falco's rule engine was inspired by Snort's but designed to operate on a much richer and more generic dataset and was plugged into the sysdig libraries. It shipped with a relatively small but useful set of rules. This initial version of Falco was largely a single-machine tool, with no ability to be deployed in a distributed way. We released it as open source because we saw a broad community need for it and, of course, because we love open source!

Expanding into Kubernetes

As the tool evolved and the community embraced it, Falco's developers expanded it into new domains of applicability. For example, in 2018 we added Kubernetes audit logs as a data source. This feature lets Falco tap into the stream of events produced by the audit log and detect misconfigurations and threats as they happen.

Creating this feature required us to improve the engine, which made Falco more flexible and better suited to a broader range of use cases.

Joining the Cloud Native Computing Foundation

In 2018 Sysdig contributed Falco to the Cloud Native Computing Foundation (CNCF) as a sandbox project. The CNCF is the home of many important projects at the foundation of modern cloud computing, such as Kubernetes, Prometheus, Envoy, and OPA. For our team, making Falco part of the CNCF was a way to evolve it into a truly community-driven effort, to make sure it would be flawlessly integrated with the rest of the cloud native stack, and to guarantee long-term support for it. In 2021 this effort was expanded by the contribution of the sysdig kernel module, eBPF probe, and libraries to the CNCF, as a subproject in the Falco organization. The full Falco stack is now in the hands of a neutral and caring community.

Plugins and the cloud

As years passed and Falco matured, a couple of things became clear. First, its sophisticated engine, efficient nature, and ease of deployment make it suitable for much more than system call–based runtime security. Second, as software becomes more and more distributed and complex, runtime security is paramount to immediately detecting threats, both expected and unexpected. Finally, we believe that the world needs a consistent, standardized way to approach runtime security. In particular, there is great demand for a solution that can protect workloads (processes, containers, services, applications) and infrastructure (hosts, networks, cloud services) in a converged way.

As a consequence, the next step in the evolution of Falco was adding modularity, flexibility, and support for many more data sources spanning different domains. For example, in 2021 a new plugin infrastructure was added that allows Falco to tap into data sources like cloud provider logs to detect misconfigurations, unauthorized access, data theft, and much more.

A long journey

Falco's story stretches across more than two decades and links many people, inventions, and projects that at first glance don't appear related. In our opinion, this story exemplifies why open source is so cool: becoming a contributor lets you learn from the smart people who came before you, build on top of their innovations, and connect communities in creative ways.

CHAPTER 2

Getting Started with Falco on Your Local Machine

Now that you're acquainted with the possibilities that Falco offers, what better way to familiarize yourself with it than to try it? In this chapter, you will discover how easy it is to install and run Falco on a local machine. We'll walk you through the process step-by-step, introducing and analyzing the core concepts and functions. We will generate an event that Falco will detect for us by simulating a malicious action, and show you how to read Falco's notification output. We'll finish the chapter by presenting some manageable approaches to customizing your installation.

Running Falco on Your Local Machine

Although Falco is not a typical application, installing and running it on a local machine is quite simple—all you need is a Linux host or a virtual machine and a terminal. There are two components to install: the user space program (named *falco*) and a driver. The driver is needed to collect system calls, which are one possible data source for Falco. For simplicity, we will focus only on system call capture in this chapter.

 You will learn more about the available drivers and why we need them to instrument the system in Chapter 3 and explore alternative data sources in Chapter 4. For the moment, you only need to know that the default driver, which is implemented as a Linux kernel module, is enough to collect system calls and start using Falco.

Several methods are available to install these components, as you will see in Chapter 8. However, in this chapter we've opted to use the binary package. It works with almost any Linux distribution and has no automation: you can touch its components with your hands. The binary package includes the *falco* program, the *falco-driver-loader* script (a utility to help you install the driver), and many other required files. You can download this package from the official website of The Falco Project (*https://falco.org*), where you'll also find comprehensive information about installing it. So, let's get to it!

Downloading and Installing the Binary Package

Falco's binary package is distributed as a single tarball compressed with GNU zip (gzip). The tarball file is named *falco-<x.y.z>-<arch>.tar.gz*, where *<x.y.z>* is the version of a Falco release and *<arch>* is the intended architecture (e.g., *x86_64*) for the package.

All the available packages are listed on Falco's "Download" page (*https://oreil.ly/Hx6Dy*). You can grab the URL of the binary package and download it locally, for example using `curl`:

```
$ curl -L -O \
    https://download.falco.org/packages/bin/x86_64/falco-0.32.0-x86_64.tar.gz
```

After downloading the tarball, uncompressing and untarring it is quite simple:

```
$ tar -xvf falco-0.32.0-x86_64.tar.gz
```

The tarball content, which you've just extracted, is intended to be copied directly to the local filesystem's root (i.e., /), without any special installation procedure. To copy it, run this command as root:

```
$ sudo cp -R falco-0.32.0-x86_64/* /
```

Now you're ready to install the driver.

Installing the Driver

System calls are Falco's default data source. To instrument the Linux kernel and collect these system calls, it needs a driver: either a Linux kernel module or an eBPF probe. The driver needs to be built for the specific version and configuration of the kernel on which Falco will run. Fortunately, The Falco Project provides literally thousands of prebuilt drivers for the vast majority of the most common Linux distributions, with various kernel versions available for download. If a prebuilt driver for your distribution and kernel version is not yet available, the files you installed in the previous section include the source code of both the kernel module and the eBPF probe, so it is also possible to build the driver locally.

This might sound like a lot, but the *falco-driver-loader* script you've just installed can do all these steps. All you need to do before using the script is install a few necessary dependencies:

- Dynamic Kernel Module Support (dkms)
- GNU make
- The Linux kernel headers

Depending on the package manager you're using, the actual package names can vary; however, they aren't difficult to find. Once you've installed these packages, you're ready to run the *falco-driver-loader* script as root. If everything goes well, the script output should look something like this:

```
$ sudo falco-driver-loader
* Running falco-driver-loader for: falco version=0.32.0, driver version=39ae...
* Running falco-driver-loader with: driver=module, compile=yes, download=yes
...
* Looking for a falco module locally (kernel 5.18.1-arch1-1)
* Trying to download a prebuilt falco module from https://download.falco.org/...
curl: (22) The requested URL returned error: 404
Unable to find a prebuilt falco module
* Trying to dkms install falco module with GCC /usr/bin/gcc
```

This output contains some useful information. The first line reports the versions of Falco and the driver that are being installed. The subsequent line tells us that the script will try to download a prebuilt driver so it can install a kernel module. If the prebuilt driver is not available, Falco will try to build it locally. The rest of the output shows the process of building and installing the module via DKMS, and finally that the module has been installed and loaded.

Starting Falco

To start Falco, you just have to run it as root:[1]

```
$ sudo falco
Mon Jun  6 16:08:29 2022: Falco version 0.32.0 (driver version 39ae7d404967...
Mon Jun  6 16:08:29 2022: Falco initialized with configuration file /etc/fa...
Mon Jun  6 16:08:29 2022: Loading rules from file /etc/falco/falco_rules.yaml:
Mon Jun  6 16:08:29 2022: Loading rules from file /etc/falco/falco_rules.loc...
Mon Jun  6 16:08:29 2022: Starting internal webserver, listening on port 8765
```

Note the configuration and rules files' paths. We'll look at these in more detail in Chapters 9 and 13. Finally, in the last line, we can see that a web server has been started; this is done because Falco exposes a health check endpoint that you can use to test that it's up and running.

---

1 Falco needs to run with root privileges to operate the driver that in turn collects system calls. However, alternative approaches are possible. For example, you can learn from Falco's "Running" page (*https://oreil.ly/6VD67*) how to run Falco in a container with the principle of least privilege.

In this chapter, to get you used to it, we have simply run Falco as an interactive shell process; therefore, a simple Ctrl-C is enough to end the process. Throughout the book, we will show you different and more sophisticated ways to install and run it.

Once Falco prints this startup information, it is ready to issue a notification whenever a condition in the loaded ruleset is met. Right now, you probably won't see any notifications (assuming nothing malicious is running on your system). In the next section, we will generate a suspicious event.

Generating Events

There are millions of ways to generate events. In the case of system calls, in reality, many events happen continuously as soon as processes are running. However, to see Falco in action, we must focus on events that can trigger an alert. As you'll recall, Falco comes preloaded with an out-of-the-box set of rules that cover the most common security scenarios. It uses rules to express unwanted behaviors, so we need to pick a rule as our target and then trigger it by simulating a malicious action within our system.

In the course of the book, and particularly in Chapter 13, you will learn about the complete anatomy of a rule, how to interpret and write a condition using Falco's rule syntax, and which fields are supported in the conditions and outputs. For the moment, let's briefly recall what a rule is and explain its structure by considering a real example:

```
- rule: Write below binary dir
  desc: an attempt to write to any file below a set of binary directories
  condition: >
    bin_dir and evt.dir = < and open_write
  output: >
    File below a known binary directory opened for writing
    (user=%user.name user_loginuid=%user.lo command=%proc.cmdline
    file=%fd.name parent=%proc.pname pcmdline=%proc.pcmdline
    gparent=%proc.aname[2] container_id=%container.id
    image=%container.image.repository)
  priority: ERROR
  source: syscall
```

A rule declaration is a YAML object with several keys. The first key, rule, uniquely identifies the rule within a *ruleset* (one or more YAML files containing rule definitions). The second key, desc, allows the rule's author to briefly describe what the rule will detect. The condition key, arguably the most important one, allows expressing a security assertion using some straightforward syntax. Various Boolean and comparison operators can be combined with *fields* (which hold the collected data) to filter only relevant events. In this example rule, `evt.dir` is a field used for filtering. Supported fields and filters are covered in more detail in Chapter 6.

As long as the condition is false, nothing will happen. The assertion is met when the condition is true, and then an alert will be fired immediately. The alert will contain an informative message, as defined by the rule's author using the `output` key of the rule declaration. The value of the `priority` key will be reported too. The content of an alert is covered in more detail in the next section.

The `condition`'s syntax can also make use of a few more constructs, like `list` and `macro`, that can be defined in the ruleset alongside rules. As the name suggests, a *list* is a list of items that can be reused across different rules. Similarly, *macros* are reusable pieces of conditions. For completeness, here are the two macros (`bin_dir` and `open_write`) utilized in the `condition` key of the *Write below binary dir* rule:

```
- macro: bin_dir
  condition: fd.directory in (/bin, /sbin, /usr/bin, /usr/sbin)

- macro: open_write
  condition: >
    evt.type in (open,openat,openat2)
    and evt.is_open_write=true
    and fd.typechar='f'
    and fd.num>=0
```

At runtime, when rules are loaded, macros expand. Consequently, we can imagine the final rule condition will be similar to:

```
    evt.type in (open,openat,openat2)
    and evt.is_open_write=true
    and fd.typechar='f'
    and fd.num>=0
    and evt.dir = <
    and fd.directory in (/bin, /sbin, /usr/bin, /usr/sbin)
```

Conditions make extensive use of fields. In this example, you can easily recognize which parts of the condition are fields (`evt.type`, `evt.is_open_write`, `fd.typechar`, `evt.dir`, `fd.num`, and `fd.directory`) since they are followed by a comparison operator (e.g., =, >=, in). Field names contain a dot (.) because fields with a similar context are grouped together in *classes*. The part before the dot represents the class (for example, `evt` and `fd` are classes).

Although you might not thoroughly understand the condition's syntax yet, you don't need to at the moment. All you need to know is that creating a file (which implies opening a file for writing) under one of the directories listed within the condition (like */bin*) should be enough to trigger the rule's condition. Let's try it.

First, start Falco with our target rule loaded. The *Write below binary dir* rule is included in */etc/falco/falco_rules.yaml*, which is loaded by default when starting Falco, so you don't need to copy it manually. Just open a terminal and run:

```
$ sudo falco
```

Second, trigger the rule by creating a file in the */bin* directory. A straightforward way to do this is by opening another terminal window and typing:

```
$ sudo touch /bin/surprise
```

Now, if you return to the first terminal with Falco running, you should find a line in the log (that is, an alert emitted by Falco) that looks like the following:

```
16:52:09.350818073: Error File below a known binary directory opened for writing
   (user=root user_loginuid=1000 command=touch /bin/surprise file=/bin/surprise
   parent=sudo pcmdline=sudo touch /bin/surprise gparent=zsh container_id=host
   image=<NA>)
```

Falco caught us! Fortunately, that's exactly what we wanted to happen. (We'll look at this output in more detail in the next section.)

Rules let us tell Falco which security policies we want to observe (expressed by the `condition` key) and which information we want to receive (specified by the `output` key) if a policy has been violated. Falco emits an alert (outputs a line of text) whenever an event meets the condition defined by a rule, so if you run the same command again, a new alert will fire.

After trying out this example, why not test some other rules by yourself? To facilitate this, the Falcosecurity organization offers a tool called *event-generator*. It's a simple command-line tool that does not require any special installation steps. You can download the latest release (*https://oreil.ly/CZGpM*) and uncompress it wherever you prefer. It comes with a collection of events that match many of the rules included in the default Falco ruleset. For example, to generate an event that meets the condition expressed by the *Read sensitive file untrusted* rule, you can type the following in a terminal window:

```
$ ./event-generator run syscall.ReadSensitiveFileUntrusted
```

Be aware that this tool might alter your system. For example, since the tool's purpose is to reproduce real malicious behavior, some actions modify files and directories such as */bin*, */etc*, and */dev*. Make sure you fully understand the purpose of this tool and its options before using it. As the online documentation (*https://oreil.ly/dL8gV*) recommends, running event-generator in a container is safer.

Interpreting Falco's Output

Let's take a closer look at the alert notification our experiment produced to see what important information it contains:

```
16:52:09.350818073: Error File below a known binary directory opened for writing
   (user=root user_loginuid=1000 command=touch /bin/surprise file=/bin/surprise
   parent=sudo pcmdline=sudo touch /bin/surprise gparent=zsh container_id=host
   image=<NA>)
```

This apparently complex line is actually composed of only three main elements separated by whitespace: a timestamp, severity level, and message. Let's examine each of these:

Timestamp
    Intuitively, the first element is the timestamp (followed by a colon: `16:52:09.350818073:`). That's when the event was generated. By default, it's displayed in the local time zone and includes nanoseconds. You can, if you like, configure Falco to display times in ISO 8601 format, including the date, nanoseconds, and timezone offset (in UTC).

Severity
    The second element indicates the severity (e.g., `Error`) of the alert, as specified by the `priority` key in the rule. It can assume one of the following values (ordered from the most to the least severe): `Emergency`, `Alert`, `Critical`, `Error`, `Warning`, `Notice`, `Informational`, or `Debug`. Falco allows us to filter out those alerts that are not important to us and thus reduce the noisiness of the output by specifying the minimum severity level we want to get alerts about. The default is `debug`, meaning all severity levels are included by default, but we can change this by altering the value of the `priority` parameter in the */etc/falco/falco.yaml* configuration file. For example, if we change the value of this parameter to `notice`, then we will not receive alerts about rules with `priority` equal to `INFORMATIONAL` or `DEBUG`.

Message
    The last and the most essential element is the message. This is a string produced according to the format specified by the `output` key. Its peculiarity lies in using placeholders, which the Falco engine replaces with the event data, as we will see in a moment.

    Normally, the `output` key of a rule begins with a brief text description to facilitate identifying the type of problem (e.g., `File below a known binary directory opened for writing`). Then it includes some placeholders (e.g., `%user.name`), which will be populated with actual values (e.g., `root`) when outputted. You can easily recognize placeholders since they start with a `%` symbol followed by one of the event's supported fields. These fields can be used in both the `condition` key and the `output` key of a Falco rule.

The beauty of this feature is that you can have a different output format for each security policy. This immediately gives you the most relevant information related to the violation, without having to navigate hundreds of fields.

Although this textual format likely includes all the information you need and is suitable for consumption by many other programs, it's not the only option for output—you can instruct Falco to output notifications in JSON format by simply changing a configuration parameter. The JSON output format has the advantage of being easily parsable by consumers. When enabled, Falco will emit as output a JSON line for each alert that will look like the following, which we've pretty-printed to improve readability:

```
{
    "output": "11:55:33.844042146: Error File below a known binary directory...",
    "priority": "Error",
    "rule": "Write below binary dir",
    "time": "2021-09-13T09:55:33.844042146Z",
    "output_fields": {
      "container.id": "host",
      "container.image.repository": null,
      "evt.time": 1631526933844042146,
      "fd.name": "/bin/surprise",
      "proc.aname[2]": "zsh",
      "proc.cmdline": "touch /bin/surprise",
      "proc.pcmdline": "sudo touch /bin/surprise",
      "proc.pname": "sudo",
      "user.loginuid": 1000,
      "user.name": "root"
    }
}
```

This output format reports the same text message as before. Additionally, each piece of information is separated into distinct JSON properties. You may also have noticed some extra data: for example, the rule identifier is present this time (`"rule": "Write below binary dir"`).

To try it right now, when starting Falco, simply pass the following flag as a command-line argument to override the default configuration:

```
$ sudo falco -o json_output=true
```

Alternatively, you can edit */etc/falco/falco.yaml* and set `json_output` to `true`. This will enable the JSON format every time Falco starts, without the flag.

Customizing Your Falco Instance

When you start Falco, it loads several files. In particular, it first loads the main (and only) configuration file, as the startup log shows:

```
Falco initialized with configuration file /etc/falco/falco.yaml
```

Falco looks for its configuration file at */etc/falco/falco.yaml*, by default. That's where the provided configuration file is installed. If desired, you can specify another configuration file path using the -c command-line argument when running Falco. Whatever file location you prefer, the configuration must be a YAML file mainly containing a collection of key/value pairs. Let's take a look at some of the available configuration options.

Rules Files

One of the most essential options, and the first you'll find in the provided configuration file, is the list of rules files to be loaded:

```
rules_file:
  - /etc/falco/falco_rules.yaml
  - /etc/falco/falco_rules.local.yaml
  - /etc/falco/rules.d
```

Despite the naming (for backward compatibility), rules_file allows you to specify multiple entries, each of which can be either a rules file or a directory containing rules files. If the entry is a file, Falco reads it directly. In the case of a directory, Falco will read every file in that directory.

The order matters here. The files are loaded in the presented order (files within a directory are loaded in alphabetical order). Users can customize predefined rules by simply overriding them in files that appear later in the list. For example, say you want to turn off the *Write below binary dir* rule, which is included in */etc/falco/falco_rules.yaml*. All you need to do is edit */etc/falco/falco_rules.local.yaml* (which appears below that file in the list and is intended to add local overrides) and write:

```
- rule: Write below binary dir
  enabled: false
```

Output Channels

There is a group of options that control Falco's available *output channels*, allowing you to specify where the security notifications should go. Furthermore, you can enable more than one simultaneously. You can easily recognize them within the configuration file (*/etc/falco/falco.yaml*) since their keys are suffixed with _output.

By default, the only two enabled output channels are `stdout_output`, which instructs Falco to send alert messages to the standard output, and `syslog_output`, which sends them to the system logging daemon. Their configurations are:

```
stdout_output:
  enabled: true

syslog_output:
  enabled: true
```

Falco provides several other advanced built-in output channels. For example:

```
file_output:
  enabled: false
  keep_alive: false
  filename: ./events.txt
```

When `file_output` is enabled, Falco will also write its alerts to the file specified by the subkey `filename`.

Other output channels allow you to consume alerts in sophisticated ways and integrate with third parties. For instance, if you want to pass the Falco output to a local program, you can use:

```
program_output:
  enabled: false
  keep_alive: false
  program: mail -s "Falco Notification" someone@example.com
```

Once you enable this, Falco will execute the program for each alert and write its content to the program's standard output. You can set the `program` subkey to any valid shell command, so this is an excellent opportunity to show off your favorite one-liners.

If you simply need to integrate with a webhook, a more convenient option is to use the `http_output` output channel:

```
http_output:
  enabled: false
  url: http://some.url
```

A simple HTTP POST request will be sent to the specified `url` for each alert. That makes it really easy to connect Falco to other tools, like Falcosidekick, which will forward alerts to Slack, Teams, Discord, Elasticsearch, and many other destinations.

Last but not least, Falco comes with a gRPC API and a corresponding output, `grpc_output`. Enabling the gRPC API and gRPC output channel allows you to connect Falco to falco-exporter, which, in turn, will export metrics to Prometheus.

Falcosidekick and falco-exporter are open source projects you can find under the Falcosecurity GitHub organization (*https://oreil.ly/ CF0Bk*). In Chapter 12, you will meet these tools again and learn how to work with outputs.

Conclusion

This chapter showed you how to install and run Falco on your local machine as a playground. You saw some simple ways to generate events and learned how to decode the output. We then looked at how to use the configuration file to customize Falco's behavior. Loading and extending rules are the primary ways to instruct Falco on what to protect. Likewise, configuring the output channels empowers us to consume notifications in ways that meet our needs.

Armed with this knowledge, you can start experimenting with Falco confidently. The rest of this book will expand on you've learned here and eventually help you master Falco completely.

PART II

The Architecture of Falco

CHAPTER 3

Understanding Falco's Architecture

Welcome to Part II of the book! In Part I, you learned what Falco is and what it does. You also took a high-level look at its architecture, installed it on your machine, and took it for a spin. Now it's time to step up your game!

In this part of the book (Chapters 3 through 8), we'll get into the inner workings of Falco. You will learn about its architecture in more detail, including its main components and how data flows across them. We'll show you how Falco interfaces with the kernel of the operating system and with the cloud logs to collect data, and how this data is enriched with context and metadata. Chapter 6 will then introduce you to the important topic of fields and filters, while Chapter 7 will get you more familiar with Falco rules. We'll conclude Part II by talking about the outputs framework, a key piece of Falco.

Do you really need to learn about the internals of Falco in order to operate it? The answer, as it is so often in life, is "it depends." If your goal is simply to deploy Falco in its default configuration and show your boss that it's up and working, then you're probably fine skipping this part of the book. However, doing so will make some things hard, and others impossible. For example, in Parts III and IV we'll cover:

- Interpreting Falco's output
- Determining if an alert could be a false positive
- Fine-tuning Falco to privilege accuracy over noise
- Precisely adapting Falco to your environment
- Customizing and extending Falco

All of these tasks require you to truly understand the core concepts behind Falco and its architecture, and that's what we'll help you accomplish here.

True security is never trivial. It requires an investment that goes beyond a superficial understanding. But that investment is typically paid back in spades, because it can make the difference in whether your software gets compromised and your company ends up in the news for all the wrong reasons.

Assuming we've convinced you, let's get started. Figure 3-1 depicts the main components of a typical Falco sensor deployment.

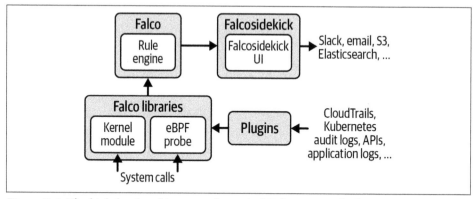

Figure 3-1. The high-level architecture of a typical Falco sensor deployment

The architecture depicted in Figure 3-1 reflects the components as they are organized at the code level in the Falcosecurity organization on GitHub (*https://oreil.ly/ClRJj*). At this level of granularity, the main components are:

Falco libraries
> The Falco libraries (*https://oreil.ly/6CbQH*), or "libs," are responsible for collecting the data the sensor will process. They also manage state and provide multiple layers of enrichment for the collected data.

Plugins
> The plugins (*https://oreil.ly/9Jyi8*) extend the sensor with additional data sources. For example, plugins make it possible for Falco to use AWS CloudTrail and Kubernetes audit logs as data sources.

Falco
> This is the main sensor executable (*https://oreil.ly/2IQkj*), including the rule engine.

Falcosidekick
> Falcosidekick (*https://oreil.ly/lmOie*) is responsible for routing the notifications and connecting the sensor to the external world.

Of the components in Figure 3-1, Falco and the Falco libs are required and always installed, while Falcosidekick and the plugins are optional; you can install them based on your deployment strategy and needs.

Falco and the Falco Libraries: A Data-Flow View

Let's take the two most important of the components we just described, the Falco libraries and Falco, and explore their data flows and critical modules.

As Figure 3-2 shows, system calls are one of the core sources of data. These are captured in the kernel of the operating system by one of Falco's two drivers: the *kernel module* and the *eBPF (extended Berkeley Packet Filter) probe*.

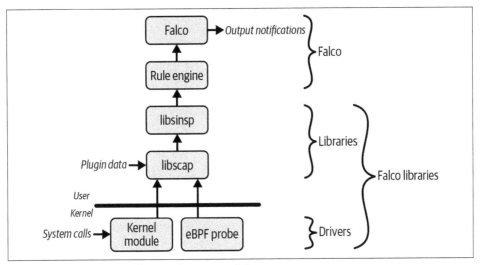

Figure 3-2. Sensor data flow and main modules

The collected system calls flow into the first of the Falco core libraries, *libscap*, which can also receive data from the plugins and exposes a common interface to the upper layers. Data is then passed to the other key library, *libsinsp*, to be parsed and enriched. Next, the data is fed to the rule engine for evaluation. Falco receives the output of the rule engine and emits the resulting notifications, which can optionally go to Falcosidekick.

Pretty straightforward, right? Figure 3-3 gives further details about what each of these modules does, and in the following sections we'll explore them in more depth.

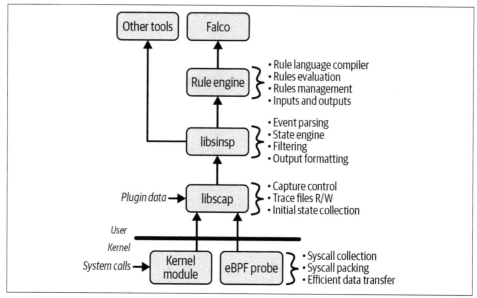

Figure 3-3. Key roles of the sensor's main modules

Drivers

System calls are Falco's original data source, and to this day they remain the most important. Collecting system calls is at the core of Falco's ability to trace the behavior of processes, containers, and users in a very granular way and with high efficiency. Reliable and efficient system call collection needs to be performed from inside the kernel of the operating system, so it requires a driver that runs inside the OS itself. As mentioned in the previous section, Falco offers two such drivers: the kernel module and the eBPF probe.

These two components offer identical functionality and are deployed in a mutually exclusive way: if you deploy the kernel module, you can't run the eBPF probe, and vice versa. So what distinguishes them?

The kernel module works with any version of the Linux kernel, including older ones. Also, it requires somewhat fewer resources to run, so you should use it when you care about Falco having the smallest possible overhead.

The eBPF probe, on the other hand, runs only on more recent versions of Linux, starting at kernel 4.11. Its advantage is that it's safer, because its code is strictly validated by the operating system before it is executed. This means that even if it contains a bug, it is (in theory) guaranteed not to crash your machine. Compared to the kernel module, it is also much better protected from security flaws that could compromise the machine where you run it. Therefore, in most cases, the eBPF probe is the option you should go with. Note also that some environments—in particular, cloud-based managed containerized environments—prevent kernel modules from being loaded in the operating system kernel. In such environments, the eBPF probe is your only option.

Both the kernel module and the eBPF probe are entrusted with a set of very important tasks:

Capturing system calls
> The driver's first responsibility is capturing system calls. This happens through a kernel facility called tracepoints (*https://oreil.ly/tEYsq*) and is heavily optimized to minimize the performance impact on the monitored applications.

System call packing
> The driver then encodes the system call information into a transfer buffer, using a format that the rest of the Falco stack can parse easily and efficiently.

Zero-copy data transfer
> Finally, the driver is responsible for efficiently transferring this data from the kernel to the user level, where *libscap* will receive it. We should really call this efficiently *not* transferring the data, since both the kernel module and the eBPF probe are designed around a zero-copy architecture that maps the data buffers into user-level memory so that *libscap* can access the original data without needing to copy or transfer it.

In Chapter 4 you will learn all you need to know about drivers, including their architecture, functionality, and usage scenarios.

Plugins

Plugins are a way to add additional data sources to Falco simply and without the need to rebuild it. Plugins implement an interface that feeds events into Falco, similar to what the kernel module and eBPF probe do. However, plugins are not limited to capturing system calls: they can feed Falco any kind of data, including logs and API events.

Falco has several powerful plugins that extend its scope. For example, the CloudTrail plugin ingests JSON logs from AWS CloudTrail and allows Falco to alert you when something dangerous happens in your cloud infrastructure. Plugins can be written in any language, but there are Go and C++ software development kits (SDKs) available that make it easier to write them in those languages. We will talk more about plugins in Chapters 4 and 11.

libscap

The name *libscap* stands for "library for system capture," a clear hint about its purpose. *libscap* is the gateway through which the input data passes before getting into the Falco processing pipeline. Let's take a look at the main things *libscap* does for us.

Managing Data Sources

The *libscap* library contains the logic to control both the kernel module and the eBPF probe, including loading them, starting and stopping captures, and reading the data they produce. It also includes the logic to load, manage, and run plugins.

libscap is designed to export a generic capture source abstraction to the upper layers of the stack. This means that no matter how you collect data (kernel module, eBPF probe, a plugin), programs that use *libscap* will have a consistent way to enumerate and control data sources, start and stop captures, and receive captured events, and you won't have to worry about the nuances of interfacing with these disparate input sources.

Supporting Trace Files

Another extremely important piece of functionality in *libscap* is support for trace files. If you've ever created or opened a PCAP file with Wireshark or tcpdump, we're sure you understand how useful (and powerful!) the concept of trace files is. If not, allow us to explain.

In addition to capturing and decoding network traffic, protocol analyzers (like Wireshark and tcpdump) let you "dump" the captured network packets into a *trace file*. The trace file contains a copy of each packet so that later you can open it to analyze the activity of that network segment. You can also share it with other people or filter its contents to isolate relevant information.

Trace files are often referred to as PCAP *files*, a name that originates from the *.pcap* file format used to encode the data inside them (an open, standardized format understood by every networking tool in the universe). This enables an endless list of the capture now, analyze later workflows that are critical in computer networks.

Many Falco users don't realize that Falco supports trace files using the *.pcap* format. This feature is extremely powerful and should definitely be part of your arsenal as you gain more experience. For example, trace files are invaluable when it comes to writing new rules.

We'll talk extensively about how to leverage trace files, for example in Chapters 4 and 13, but for now let's whet your appetite by teaching you how to create a trace file and have Falco read it, in two simple steps. To do that, we need to introduce a command-line tool called sysdig. You'll learn more about sysdig in Chapter 4, but for the moment we'll just use it as a simple trace file generator.

Step 1: Create the trace file

Install sysdig on your Linux host by following the installation instructions (*https://oreil.ly/Rmkxr*). After finishing the installation, run the following on your command line, which instructs sysdig to capture all of the system calls generated by the host and write them to a file called *testfile.scap*:

```
$ sudo sysdig -w testfile.scap
```

Wait a few seconds to make sure your machine is working on it, then press Ctrl-C to stop sysdig.

Now you have a snapshot of a few seconds' worth of your host's activity. Let's take a look at what it contains:

```
$ sysdig -r testfile.scap
1 17:41:13.628568857 0 prlcp (4358) < write res=0 data=.N;.n...
2 17:41:13.628573305 0 prlcp (4358) > write fd=6(<p>pipe:[43606]) size=1
3 17:41:13.628588359 0 prlcp (4358) < write res=1 data=.
4 17:41:13.609136030 3 gmain (2935) < poll res=0 fds=
5 17:41:13.609146818 3 gmain (2935) > write fd=4(<e>) size=8
6 17:41:13.609149203 3 gmain (2935) < write res=8 data=........
7 17:41:13.609151765 3 gmain (2935) > read fd=7(<i>) size=4096
8 17:41:13.609153301 3 gmain (2935) < read res=-11(EAGAIN) data=
9 17:41:13.626956525 0 Xorg (3214) < epoll_wait res=1
10 17:41:13.626964759 0 Xorg (3214) > setitimer
11 17:41:13.626966955 0 Xorg (3214) < setitimer
12 17:41:13.626969972 0 Xorg (3214) > recvmsg fd=42(<u>@/tmp/.X11-unix/X0)
13 17:41:13.626976118 0 Xorg (3214) < recvmsg res=28 size=28 data=....E..... ...
14 17:41:13.626992585 0 Xorg (3214) > writev fd=42(<u>@/tmp/.X11-unix/X0) size=32
15 17:41:13.627013409 0 Xorg (3214) < writev res=32 data=...7E.............. ...

...
```

We'll go through the format of this output in detail later, but you can probably tell that this is a bunch of background input/output (I/O) activity performed by system tools like Xorg, gmain, and prlcp, which are running on this machine while it's idle.

Step 2: Process the trace file with Falco

Think of the trace file as taking us back in time: you took a snapshot of your host at a specific point in time, and now you can trace the system calls generated on the host around that time, observing every process in detail. Processing the trace file with

Falco is easy and lets you see quickly if any security violations happened during that time. Here's a sample of its output:

```
$ falco -e testfile.scap
Wed Sep 29 18:04:00 2021: Falco version 0.30.0
Wed Sep 29 18:04:00 2021: Falco initialized with configuration file /etc/falco
/falco.yaml
Wed Sep 29 18:04:00 2021: Loading rules from file /etc/falco/falco_rules.yaml:
Wed Sep 29 18:04:00 2021: Reading system call events from file: testfile.scap
Events detected: 0
Rule counts by severity:
Triggered rules by rule name:
Syscall event drop monitoring:
   - event drop detected: 0 occurrences
   - num times actions taken: 0
```

Fortunately, it looks like we're safe. This consistent, back-in-time way of running Falco is useful when writing or unit-testing rules. We'll talk more about it when we deep dive into rules in Chapter 13.

Collecting System State

System state collection is an important task that's specifically related to capturing system calls. The kernel module and the eBPF probe produce raw system calls, which lack some important context Falco needs.

Let's take a look at an example. A very common system call is read, which, as the name implies, reads a buffer of data from a file descriptor. Here is the prototype of read:

```
ssize_t read(int fd, void *buf, size_t count);
```

It has three inputs: the numeric file descriptor identifier, a buffer to fill, and the buffer size. It returns the amount of data that was written in the buffer.

A *file descriptor* is like the ID of an object inside the operating system kernel: it can indicate a file, a network connection (specifically, a socket), the endpoint of a pipe, a mutex (used for process synchronization), a timer, or several other types of objects.

Knowing the file descriptor number is not very useful when crafting a Falco rule. As users, we prefer to think about a file or directory name, or maybe a connection's IP addresses and ports, than a file descriptor number. *libscap* helps us do that. When Falco starts, *libscap* fetches a bunch of data from a diverse set of sources within the operating system (for example, the */proc* Linux filesystem). It uses this data to construct a set of tables that can be used to resolve cryptic numbers—file descriptors, process IDs, and so forth—into logical entities and their details, which are much easier for humans to use.

This functionality is part of why Falco's syntax is so much more expressive and usable than that of most comparable tools. One theme that you will be hearing often in this book is that *granular data is useless without context*. This gives you a hint of what that means. Next we'll dive into the other important Falco library: *libsinsp*.

libsinsp

libsinsp stands for "library for system inspection." This library taps into the stream of data *libscap* produces, enriches it, and provides a number of higher-level primitives to work with it. Let's start by exploring its most important functionality, the state engine.

State Engine

As we noted in the previous section, when Falco starts, *libscap* constructs a set of tables to convert low-level identifiers, like file descriptor numbers, into high-level, actionable information, like IP addresses and filenames. This is great, but what if a program opens a file *after* Falco starts? For example, a very common system call in Unix is open, which takes two input arguments, the filename and some flags, and returns a file descriptor identifying the newly opened file:

```
int open(const char *pathname, int flags);
```

In practice, open, like many other system calls, creates a new file descriptor, effectively changing the state of the process that called it. If a process invokes open after Falco has been launched, its new file descriptor will not be part of the state table, and Falco won't know what to do with that descriptor. However, consider this: open is a system call. More generally, system calls are always used to create, destroy, or modify file descriptors. Recall, too, that the Falco libs capture *all* system calls from *every* process.

libsinsp, in particular, has logic to inspect every state-changing system call and, based on the system call arguments, update the state tables. In other words, it tracks the activity of the whole machine to keep the state in sync with the underlying operating system. Further, it does so in a way that accurately supports containers. *libsinsp* keeps this constantly updated information in a hierarchical structure. This structure (Figure 3-4) starts with a process table, each entry of which contains a file descriptor table, among other information.

These accurate, constantly updated state tables are at the core of Falco's data enrichment, which in turn is a key building block of the rule engine.

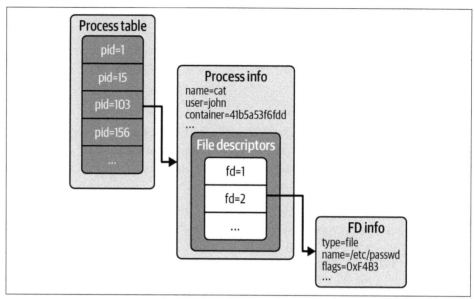

Figure 3-4. The libsinsp state hierarchy

Event Parsing

The state engine requires a substantial amount of logic to understand system calls and parse their arguments. This is what *libsinsp*'s *event parser* does. State tracking leverages event parsing, but it's used for other purposes as well. For example, it extracts useful arguments from system calls or other data sources, making them available to the rule engine. It also collates and reconstructs buffers that can be spread across multiple collected messages, making it easier to decode their content from Falco rules.

Filtering

Filtering is one of the most important concepts in Falco, and it's fully implemented in *libsinsp*. A *filter* is a Boolean expression that ties together multiple *checks*, each of which compares a filter field with a constant value. The importance of filters is obvious when we look at rules. (Indeed, it's so important that we dedicate all of Chapter 6 to it.) Let's take the simple rule shown here:

```
- rule: shell_in_container
  desc: shell opened inside a container
  condition: container.id != host and proc.name = bash
  output: shell in a container (user=%user.name container_id=%container.id)
  priority: WARNING
```

The `condition` section of the rule is a *libsinsp* filter. The condition in our example checks that the container ID is not `host` and that the name of the process is `bash`. Every captured system call that meets both criteria will trigger the rule.

libsinsp is responsible for defining and implementing system call–related filter fields. It also contains the engine that evaluates filters and tells us if the rule should trigger, so it's not an exaggeration to say that *libsinsp* is the heart of Falco.

Output Formatting

If we take another look at the example rule, we can see that the `output` section makes use of a syntax similar to that of the `condition` section:

```
output: shell in a container (user=%user.name container_id=%container.id)
```

Output is what Falco prints when the rule triggers—and yes, you can use filter fields in this section (the same fields that you can use in the `condition` section) by prepending the % character to the field names. *libsinsp* has logic to resolve these fields and create the final output string. What's nice is that if you become an expert at writing condition filters, you will also have mastered output strings!

One More Thing About libsinsp

By now you can probably see that a lot of Falco's logic is in *libsinsp*. That's deliberate. Falco's developers recognized the value (and elegance) of its data collection stack and realized it could be the base for many other tools. That's precisely why *libsinsp* exists. It sits on top of the powerful Falco collection stack (which includes the drivers, plugins, and *libscap*) and adds the most important pieces of the Falco logic in a way that makes them reusable. What's more, *libsinsp* includes all you need to collect security and forensics data from containers, virtual machines, Linux hosts, and cloud infrastructure. It's stable, efficient, and well documented.

Several other open source and commercial tools have been built on top of *libsinsp*. If you would like to write one, or if you are just curious and want to learn more, we recommend you start at the *falcosecurity/libs* repository (*https://oreil.ly/Cp2Nt*).

Rule Engine

The Falco rule engine is the component you interact with when you run Falco. Here are some of the things that the rule engine is responsible for:

- Loading Falco rules files
- Parsing the rules in a file
- Applying local customizations (such as appends and overrides) to rules based on local rules files

- Using *libsinsp* to compile the condition and output of each rule
- Performing the appropriate action, including emitting the output, when a rule triggers

Thanks to the power of *libscap* and *libsinsp*, the rule engine is simple and relatively independent from the rest of the stack.

Conclusion

Now you know what's inside Falco and how its components relate to each other—you're well on your way to mastering it! In the next chapters we'll dive deeper into some of the components and concepts that this chapter introduced.

CHAPTER 4

Data Sources

In this chapter we'll take a deep dive into the kernel of the operating system and Falco's data collection stack. You'll learn how Falco captures the different types of events that feed its rule engine, how its data collection process compares to alternative approaches, and why it was built the way it is. You'll get to understand the details well enough that you will be able to pick and deploy the right drivers and plugins for your needs by the end of this chapter.

The first order of business is understanding what data sources you can use in Falco. Falco's data sources can be grouped into two main families: system calls and plugins. System calls are Falco's original data source. They come from the kernel of the operating system and offer visibility into the activities of processes, containers, virtual machines, and hosts. Falco uses them to protect workloads and applications. The second family of data sources, plugins, is relatively new: support was added in 2022. Plugins connect various types of inputs to Falco, such as cloud logs and APIs.

Falco previously supported Kubernetes audit logs as a third, separate source type; starting from Falco 0.32, however, this data source has been reimplemented as a plugin, so we won't cover it in this chapter.

System Calls

As we've stated several times already, system calls are a key source of data for Falco and one of the ingredients that make it unique. But what exactly is a system call? Let's start with a high-level definition, courtesy of Wikipedia (*https://oreil.ly/pbS0B*):

> In computing, a system call (commonly abbreviated to syscall) is the programmatic way in which a computer program requests a service from the kernel of the operating system on which it is executed. This may include hardware-related services (for example, accessing a hard disk drive or accessing the device's camera), creation and

execution of new processes, and communication with integral kernel services such as process scheduling.

Let's unpack this. At the highest level of abstraction, a computer consists of a bunch of hardware that runs a bunch of software. In modern computing, however, it's extremely unusual for a program to run directly on the hardware. Instead, in the vast majority of cases, programs run on top of an operating system. Falco's drivers focus specifically on the operating system powering the cloud and the modern data center: Linux.

An *operating system* is a piece of software designed to conduct and support the execution of other software. Among many other things, the OS takes care of:

- Scheduling processes
- Managing memory
- Mediating hardware access
- Implementing network connectivity
- Handling concurrency

Clearly, the vast majority of this functionality needs to be exposed to the programs that are running on top of the OS, so that they can do something useful. And clearly, the best way for a piece of software to expose functionality is to offer an *application programming interface* (API): a set of functions that client programs can call. This is what system calls *almost* are: APIs to interact with the operating system.

Wait, why almost?

Well, the operating system is a unique piece of software, and you can't just call it like you would a library. The OS runs in a separate execution mode, called privileged mode, that's isolated from user mode, which is the context used for executing regular processes (that is, running programs). This separation makes calling the OS more complicated. With some CPUs, you invoke a system call by triggering an interrupt. With most modern CPUs, however, you need to use a specific CPU instruction. If we exclude this additional level of complexity, it is fair to say that system calls are APIs to access operating system functionality. There are lots of them, each with their own input arguments and return value.

Every program, with no exceptions, makes extensive and constant use of the system call interface for anything that is not pure computation: reading input, generating output, accessing the disk, communicating on the network, running a new program, and so on. This means, as you can imagine, that observing system calls gives a very detailed picture of what each process does.

Operating system developers have long treated the system call interface as a stable API. This means that you can expect it to stay the same even if, inside, the kernel changes dramatically. This is important because it guarantees consistency across time and execution environments, making the system call API an ideal choice for collecting reliable security signals. Falco rules, for example, can reference specific system calls and assume that using them will work on any Linux distribution.

Examples

Linux offers *many* system calls—more than 300 of them. Going over all of them would be next to impossible and very boring, so we'll spare you that. However, we do want to give you an idea of the kinds of system calls that are available.

Table 4-1 includes some of the system call categories that are most relevant for a security tool like Falco. For each category, the table includes examples of representative system calls. You can find more information on each by entering `man 2 X`, where *X* is the system call name, in a Linux terminal or in your browser's search bar.

Table 4-1. Noteworthy system call categories

Category	Examples
File I/O	`open`, `creat`, `close`, `read`, `write`, `ioctl`, `link`, `unlink`, `chdir`, `chmod`, `stat`, `seek`, `mount`, `rename`, `mkdir`, `rmdir`
Network	`socket`, `bind`, `connect`, `listen`, `accept`, `sendto`, `recvfrom`, `getsockopt`, `setsockopt`, `shutdown`
Interprocess communication	`pipe`, `futex`, `inotify_add_watch`, `eventfd`, `semop`, `semget`, `semctl`, `msgctl`
Process management	`clone`, `execve`, `fork`, `nice`, `kill`, `prctl`, `exit`, `setrlimit`, `setpriority`, `capset`
Memory management	`brk`, `mmap`, `mprotect`, `mlock`, `madvise`
User management	`setuid`, `getuid`, `setgid`, `getgid`
System	`sethostname`, `setdomainname`, `reboot`, `syslog`, `uname`, `swapoff`, `init_module`, `delete_module`

> If you are interested in taking a look at the full list of Linux system calls, type `man syscalls` into a Linux terminal or a search engine. This will show the official Linux manual page, which includes a comprehensive list of system calls with hyperlinks to take a deeper look at many of them. In addition, software engineer Filippo Valsorda offers a nicely organized and searchable list (*https://oreil.ly/P12lw*) on his personal home page.

Observing System Calls

Given how crucial system calls are for Falco and for runtime security in general, it's important that you learn how to capture, observe, and interpret them. This is a valuable skill that you will find useful in many situations. We're going to show you two different tools you can use for this purpose: strace and sysdig.

strace

strace is a tool that you can expect to find on pretty much every machine running a Unix-compatible operating system. In its simplest form, you use it to run a program, and it will print every system call issued by the program to standard error. In other words, add **strace** to the beginning of an arbitrary command line and you will see all of the system calls that command line generates:

```
$ strace echo hello world
execve("/bin/echo", ["echo", "hello", "world"], 0x7ffc87eed490 /* 32 vars */) = 0
brk(NULL)                               = 0x558ba22bf000
access("/etc/ld.so.nohwcap", F_OK)      = -1 ENOENT (No such file or directory)
access("/etc/ld.so.preload", R_OK)      = -1 ENOENT (No such file or directory)
openat(AT_FDCWD, "/etc/ld.so.cache", O_RDONLY|O_CLOEXEC) = 3
fstat(3, {st_mode=S_IFREG|0644, st_size=121726, ...}) = 0
mmap(NULL, 121726, PROT_READ, MAP_PRIVATE, 3, 0) = 0x7f289009c000
close(3)                                = 0
access("/etc/ld.so.nohwcap", F_OK)      = -1 ENOENT (No such file or directory)
openat(AT_FDCWD, "/lib/x86_64-linux-gnu/libc.so.6", O_RDONLY|O_CLOEXEC) = 3
read(3, "\177ELF\2\1\1\3\0\0\0\0\0\0\0\0\3\0>\0\1\0\0\0\20\35\2\0\0\0\0\0" ...
fstat(3, {st_mode=S_IFREG|0755, st_size=2030928, ...}) = 0
mmap(NULL, 8192, PROT_READ|PROT_WRITE, MAP_PRIVATE|MAP_ANONYMOUS, -1, 0) ...
mmap(NULL, 4131552, PROT_READ|PROT_EXEC, MAP_PRIVATE|MAP_DENYWRITE, 3, 0) ...
mprotect(0x7f288fc87000, 2097152, PROT_NONE) = 0
mmap(0x7f288fe87000, 24576, PROT_READ|PROT_WRITE, MAP_PRIVATE|MAP_FIXED| ...
mmap(0x7f288fe8d000, 15072, PROT_READ|PROT_WRITE, MAP_PRIVATE|MAP_FIXED| ...
close(3)                                = 0
arch_prctl(ARCH_SET_FS, 0x7f289009b540) = 0
mprotect(0x7f288fe87000, 16384, PROT_READ) = 0
mprotect(0x558ba2028000, 4096, PROT_READ) = 0
mprotect(0x7f28900ba000, 4096, PROT_READ) = 0
munmap(0x7f289009c000, 121726)          = 0
brk(NULL)                               = 0x558ba22bf000
brk(0x558ba22e0000)                     = 0x558ba22e0000
openat(AT_FDCWD, "/usr/lib/locale/locale-archive", O_RDONLY|O_CLOEXEC) = 3
fstat(3, {st_mode=S_IFREG|0644, st_size=3004224, ...}) = 0
mmap(NULL, 3004224, PROT_READ, MAP_PRIVATE, 3, 0) = 0x7f288f7c2000
close(3)                                = 0
fstat(1, {st_mode=S_IFCHR|0620, st_rdev=makedev(136, 2), ...}) = 0
write(1, "hello world\n", 12hello world
)           = 12
close(1)                                = 0
close(2)                                = 0
exit_group(0)                           = ?
+++ exited with 0 +++
```

Note how strace's output mimics C syntax and looks like a stream of function invocations, with the addition of the return value after the = symbol at the end of each

---

line. For example, take a look at the `write` syscall (in bold) that outputs the "hello world" string to standard output (file descriptor 1). It returns the value 12, which is the number of bytes that have been successfully written. Note how the string "hello world" is printed to standard output *before* the `write` system call returns and strace prints its return value on the screen.

A second way to use strace is pointing it to a running process by specifying the process ID (PID) on the command line:

```
$ sudo strace -p`pidof vi`
strace: Process 16472 attached
select(1, [0], [], [0], NULL)           = 1 (in [0])
read(0, "\r", 250)                      = 1
select(1, [0], [], [0], {tv_sec=0, tv_usec=0}) = 0 (Timeout)
select(1, [0], [], [0], {tv_sec=0, tv_usec=0}) = 0 (Timeout)
write(1, "\7", 1)                       = 1
select(1, [0], [], [0], {tv_sec=4, tv_usec=0}) = 0 (Timeout)
select(1, [0], [], [0], NULL
^C
strace: Process 16472 detached
<detached ...>
```

strace has some pros and some cons. It's broadly supported, so either it's already available or it's an easy package install away. It's also simple to use and ideal when you need to inspect a single process, which makes it perfect for debugging use cases.

As for disadvantages, strace instruments individual processes, which makes it unsuitable for inspecting the activity of the whole system or when you don't have a specific process to start from. Further, strace is based on ptrace for system call collection, which makes it very slow and unsuitable for use in production environments. You should expect a process to slow down substantially (sometimes by orders of magnitude) when you attach strace to it.

sysdig

We introduced sysdig in Chapter 3's discussion of trace files. sysdig is more sophisticated than strace and includes several advanced features. While this can make it a bit harder to use, the good news is that sysdig shares Falco's data model, output format, and filtering syntax—so you can use a lot of what you learn about Falco in sysdig, and vice versa.

The first thing to keep in mind is that you don't point sysdig to an individual process like you do with strace. Instead, you just run it and it will capture every system call invoked on the machine, inside or outside containers:

```
$ sudo sysdig
1 17:41:13.628568857 0 prlcp (4358) < write res=0 data=.N;.n...
2 17:41:13.628573305 0 prlcp (4358) > write fd=6(<p>pipe:[43606]) size=1
4 17:41:13.609136030 3 gmain (2935) < poll res=0 fds=
```

```
5 17:41:13.609146818 3 gmain (2935) > write fd=4(<e>) size=8
6 17:41:13.609149203 3 gmain (2935) < write res=8 data=........
9 17:41:13.626956525 0 Xorg (3214) < epoll_wait res=1
10 17:41:13.626964759 0 Xorg (3214) > setitimer
11 17:41:13.626966955 0 Xorg (3214) < setitimer
```

Usually this is too noisy and not very useful, so you can restrict what sysdig shows you by using filters. sysdig accepts the same filtering syntax as Falco (which, incidentally, makes it a great tool to test and troubleshoot Falco rules). Here's an example where we restrict sysdig to capturing system calls for processes named "cat":

```
$ sudo sysdig proc.name=cat & cat /etc/hosts
47190 14:40:39.913809700 12 cat (377163.377163) < execve res=0 exe=cat
args=/etc/hosts. tid=377163(cat) pid=377163(cat) ptid=5860(zsh) cwd=
fdlimit=1024 pgft_maj=0 pgft_min=60 vm_size=424 vm_rss=4 vm_swap=0 comm=cat
cgroups=cpuset=/user.slice.cpu=/user.slice.cpuacct=/.io=/user.slice.memory=
/user.slic... env=SYSTEMD_EXEC_PID=3558.GJS_DEBUG_TOPICS=JS ERROR;JS
LOG.SESSION_MANAGER=local/... tty=34817 pgid=377163(cat) loginuid=1000 flags=0
47194 14:40:39.913846153 12 cat (377163.377163) > brk addr=0
47196 14:40:39.913846951 12 cat (377163.377163) < brk res=55956998C000
vm_size=424 vm_rss=4 vm_swap=0
47205 14:40:39.913880404 12 cat (377163.377163) > arch_prctl
47206 14:40:39.913880871 12 cat (377163.377163) < arch_prctl
47207 14:40:39.913896493 12 cat (377163.377163) > access mode=4(R_OK)
47208 14:40:39.913900922 12 cat (377163.377163) < access res=-2(ENOENT)
name=/etc/ld.so.preload
47209 14:40:39.913903872 12 cat (377163.377163) > openat dirfd=-100(AT_FDCWD)
name=/etc/ld.so.cache flags=4097(O_RDONLY|O_CLOEXEC) mode=0
47210 14:40:39.913914652 12 cat (377163.377163) < openat
fd=3(<f>/etc/ld.so.cache) dirfd=-100(AT_FDCWD) name=/etc/ld.so.cache
flags=4097(O_RDONLY|O_CLOEXEC) mode=0 dev=803
```

This output requires a little more explanation than strace's. The fields sysdig prints are:

- Incremental event number
- Event timestamp
- CPU ID
- Command name
- Process ID and thread ID (TID), separated by a dot
- Event direction (> means *enter*, while < means *exit*)
- Event type (for our purposes, this is the system call name)
- System call arguments

Unlike strace, sysdig prints *two* lines for each system call: the *enter* line is generated when the system call starts and the *exit* line is printed when the system call returns.

This approach works well if you need to identify how long a system call took to run or pinpoint a process that is stuck in a system call.

Also note that, by default, sysdig prints thread IDs in addition to process IDs. *Threads* are the core execution unit for the operating system and thus for sysdig as well. Multiple threads can exist within the same process or command and share resources, such as memory. The TID is the basic identifier to follow when tracking execution activity in your machine. You do that by just looking at the TID number, or by filtering out the noise with a command line like this one:

```
$ sysdig thread.tid=1234
```

which will preserve the execution flow only for thread 1234.

Threads live inside processes, which are identified by a process ID. A lot of the processes running on an average Linux box are single-threaded, and in that case `thread.tid` is the same as `proc.pid`. Filtering by `proc.pid` is useful to observe how threads interact with each other inside a process.

Trace files

As you learned in Chapter 3, you can instruct sysdig to save the system calls it captures to a trace file, like so:

```
$ sudo sysdig -w testfile.scap
```

You will likely want to use a filter to keep the file size under control. For example:

```
$ sudo sysdig -w testfile.scap proc.name=cat
```

You can also use filters when reading trace files:

```
$ sysdig -r testfile.scap proc.name=cat
```

sysdig's filters are important enough that we will devote a full chapter (Chapter 6) to them.

We recommend you play with sysdig and explore the activity of common programs in Linux. This will be helpful later, when creating or interpreting Falco rules.

Capturing System Calls

All right, system calls are cool and we need to capture them. So what's the best way to do it?

Earlier in this chapter, we described how system calls involve transitioning the execution flow from a running process to the kernel of the operating system. Intuitively, and as shown in Figure 4-1, there are two places where system calls can be captured: in the running process or the operating system kernel.

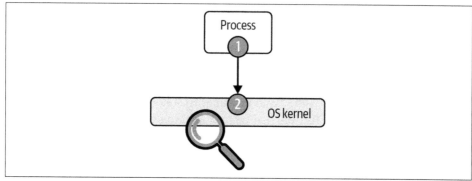

Figure 4-1. System call capture options

Capturing system calls in a running process typically involves modifying either the process or some of its libraries with some kind of instrumentation. The fact that most programs in Linux use the C standard library, also known as *glibc*, to execute system calls makes instrumenting it quite appealing. As a consequence, there are abundant tools and frameworks to modify *glibc* (and other system libraries) for instrumentation purposes. These techniques can be static, changing the library's source code and recompiling it, or dynamic, finding its location in the address space of the target process and inserting hooks in it.

 Another method to capture system calls without instrumenting the OS kernel involves using the operating system's debugging facilities. For example, strace uses a facility called *ptrace*,[1] which is at the base of tools like the GNU debugger (gdb).

The second option involves intercepting the system call execution after it has transitioned to the operating system. This requires running some code in the OS kernel itself. It tends to be more delicate and riskier, because running code in the kernel requires elevated privileges. Anything running in the kernel has potential control of the machine, its processes, its users, and its hardware. Therefore, a bug in anything that runs inside the kernel can cause major security risks, data corruption, or, in some cases, even a machine crash. This is why many security tools pick instrumentation option 1 and capture system calls at the user level, inside the process.

Falco does the opposite: it sits squarely on the kernel instrumentation side. The rationale behind this choice can be summarized in three words: accuracy, performance, and scalability. Let's explore each in turn.

---

1 Run **man 2 ptrace** for more information on this.

Accuracy

User-level instrumentation techniques—in particular, those that work at the *glibc* level—have a couple of major problems. First, a motivated attacker can evade them by, well, not using *glibc*! You don't *have* to use a library to issue system calls, and attackers can easily craft a simple sequence of CPU instructions instead, completely bypassing the *glibc* instrumentation. Not good.

Even worse, there are major categories of software that just don't load *glibc* at all. For example, statically linked C programs, very common in containers, import *glibc* functions at compile time and embed them in their executables. With these programs, you don't have the option to replace or modify the library. The same goes for programs written in Go, which has its own statically linked system call interface library.

Kernel-level capture doesn't suffer from these limitations. It supports any language, any stack, and any framework, because system call collection happens at a level below all of the libraries and abstraction layers. This means that kernel-level instrumentation is much harder for attackers to evade.

Performance

Some user-level capture techniques, such as using ptrace, have significant overhead because they generate a high number of context switches. Every single system call needs to be uniquely delivered to a separate process, which requires the execution to ping-pong between processes. This is very, very slow, to the point that it becomes an impediment to using such techniques in production, where such a substantial impact on the instrumented processes is not acceptable.

It's true that *glibc*-based capture can be more efficient, but it still introduces high overhead for basic operations like timestamping events. Kernel-level capture, by contrast, requires zero context switches and can collect all of the necessary context, like timestamps, from within the kernel. This makes it much faster than any other technique, and thus the most suitable for production.

Scalability

As the name implies, process-level capture requires "doing something" for every single process. What that something is can vary, but it still introduces an overhead that is proportional to the number of observed processes. That's not the case with kernel-level instrumentation. Take a look at Figure 4-2.

If you insert kernel instrumentation in the right place, it is possible to have one single instrumentation point (labeled 2 in Figure 4-2), no matter how many processes are running. This ensures not only maximum efficiency but also the certainty that you will never miss anything, because no process escapes kernel-level capture.

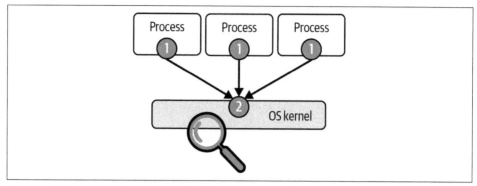

Figure 4-2. System call capture scalability, process-level versus kernel

So What About Stability and Security?

We mentioned that kernel-level instrumentation is more delicate, because a bug can cause serious problems. You might wonder, "Am I taking additional risk by choosing a tool like Falco, which is based on kernel instrumentation, instead of a product based on user-level instrumentation?"

Not really. First of all, kernel-level instrumentation benefits from well-documented, stable hooking interfaces, while approaches like *glibc*-based capture are less clean and intrinsically riskier. They cannot crash the machine, but they can absolutely crash the instrumented process, with results that are typically bad. In addition to that, technologies like eBPF greatly reduce the risk involved in running code in the kernel, making kernel-level instrumentation viable even for risk-averse users.

Kernel-Level Instrumentation Approaches

We hope we've convinced you that, whenever it's available, kernel instrumentation is the way to go for runtime security. The question now becomes, what is the best mechanism to implement it? Among the different available approaches, two are relevant for a tool like Falco: kernel modules or eBPF probes. Let's take a look at each of these approaches.

Kernel modules

Loadable kernel modules are pieces of code that can be loaded into the kernel at runtime. Historically, modules have been heavily used in Linux (and many other operating systems) to make the kernel extensible, efficient, and smaller.

Kernel modules extend the kernel's functionality without the need to reboot the system. They are typically used to implement device drivers, network protocols, and filesystems. Kernel modules are written in C and are compiled for the specific kernel inside which they will run. In other words, it's not possible to compile a module on one machine and then use it on another one (unless they have exactly the same kernel). Kernel modules can also be unloaded when the user doesn't need them anymore, to save memory.

Linux has supported kernel modules for a very long time, so they work even with very old versions of Linux. They also have extensive access to the kernel, which means there are very few restrictions on what they can do. That makes them a great choice to collect the detailed information required by a runtime security tool like Falco. Since they are written in C, kernel modules are also very efficient and therefore a great option when performance is important.

If you want to see the list of modules that are loaded in your Linux box, use this command:

```
$ sudo lsmod
```

eBPF

As mentioned in Chapter 1, eBPF is the "next generation" of the Berkeley Packet Filter (BPF). BPF was designed in 1992 for network packet filtering with BSD operating systems, and it is still used today by tools like Wireshark. BPF's innovation was the ability to execute arbitrary code in the kernel of the operating system. Since such code has more or less unlimited privileges on the machine, however, this is potentially risky and must be done with care.

Figure 4-3 shows how BPF safely runs arbitrary packet filters in the kernel.

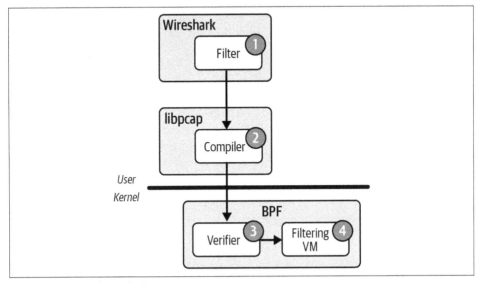

Figure 4-3. BPF filter deployment steps

Let's take a look at the steps depicted here:

1. The user inputs a filter in a program like Wireshark (e.g., `port 80`).
2. The filter is fed to a compiler, which converts it into bytecode for a virtual machine. This is conceptually similar to compiling a Java program, but both the program and the virtual machine (VM) instruction set are much simpler when using BPF. Here, for example, is what our `port 80` filter becomes after being compiled:

```
(000) ldh      [12]
(001) jeq      #0x86dd          jt 2     jf 10
(002) ldb      [20]
(003) jeq      #0x84            jt 6     jf 4
(004) jeq      #0x6             jt 6     jf 5
(005) jeq      #0x11            jt 6     jf 23
(006) ldh      [54]
(007) jeq      #0x50            jt 22    jf 8
(008) ldh      [56]
(009) jeq      #0x50            jt 22    jf 23
(010) jeq      #0x800           jt 11    jf 23
(011) ldb      [23]
(012) jeq      #0x84            jt 15    jf 13
(013) jeq      #0x6             jt 15    jf 14
(014) jeq      #0x11            jt 15    jf 23
(015) ldh      [20]
(016) jset     #0x1fff          jt 23    jf 17
(017) ldxb     4*([14]&0xf)
(018) ldh      [x + 14]
(019) jeq      #0x50            jt 22    jf 20
(020) ldh      [x + 16]
(021) jeq      #0x50            jt 22    jf 23
(022) ret      #262144
(023) ret      #0
```

3. To prevent a compiled filter from doing damage, it is analyzed by a verifier before being injected into the kernel. The verifier examines the bytecode and determines if the filter has dangerous attributes (for example, infinite loops that would cause the filter to never return, consuming a lot of kernel CPU).
4. If the filter code is not safe, the verifier rejects it, returns an error to the user, and stops the loading process. If the verifier is happy, the bytecode is delivered to the virtual machine, which runs it against every incoming packet.

eBPF is a more recent (and much more capable) version of BPF, added to Linux in 2014 and first included with kernel version 3.18. eBPF takes BPF's concepts to new levels, delivering more efficiency and taking advantage of newer hardware.

Most importantly, with hooks throughout the kernel, eBPF enables use cases that go beyond simple packet filtering, such as tracing, performance analysis, debugging, and security. It's essentially a general-purpose code execution VM that guarantees the programs it runs won't cause damage.

Here are some of the improvements that eBPF introduces over classic BPF:

- A more advanced instruction set, which means eBPF can run much more sophisticated programs.
- A just-in-time (JIT) compiler. While classic BPF was interpreted, eBPF programs, after being validated, are converted into native CPU instructions. This means they run much faster, at close to native CPU speeds.
- The ability to write real C programs instead of just simple packet filters.
- A mature set of libraries that let you control eBPF from languages like Go.
- The ability to run subprograms and helper functions.
- Safe access to several kernel objects. eBPF programs can safely "peek" into kernel structures to collect information and context, which are gold for tools like Falco.
- The concept of *maps*, memory areas that can be used to exchange data with the user level efficiently and easily.
- A much more sophisticated verifier, which lets eBPF programs do more while preserving their safety.
- The ability to run in many more places in the kernel than the network stack, using facilities like tracepoints, kprobes, uprobes, Linux Security Modules hooks, and Userland Statically Defined Tracing (USDT).

eBPF is evolving quickly and is rapidly becoming the standard way to extend the Linux kernel. eBPF scripts are flexible and safe and run extremely fast, making them perfect for capturing runtime activity.

The Falco Drivers

Falco offers two different driver implementations that implement both the approaches we just described: a kernel module and an eBPF probe. The two implementations have the same functionality and are interchangeable when using Falco. Therefore, we can describe how they work without focusing on a specific one.

The high-level capture flow is shown in Figure 4-4.

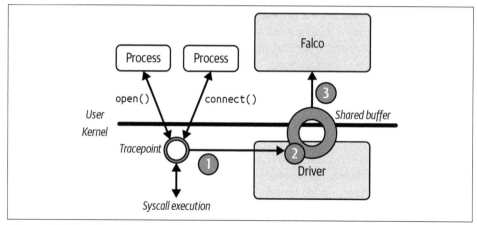

Figure 4-4. The driver's capture flow

The approach used by the Falco drivers to capture a system call involves three main steps, labeled in the figure:

1. A kernel facility called a tracepoint intercepts the execution of the system call. The tracepoint makes it possible to insert a hook at a specific place in the operating system kernel so that a callback function will be called every time kernel execution reaches that point.[2] The Falco drivers install two tracepoints for system calls: one where system calls enter the kernel, and another one where they exit the kernel and give control back to the caller process.

2. While in the tracepoint callback, the driver "packs" the system call arguments into a shared memory buffer. During this phase, the system call is also time-stamped and additional context is collected from the operating system (for example, the thread ID, or the connection details for some socket syscalls). This phase needs to be super-efficient, because the system call cannot be executed until the driver's tracepoint callback returns.

3. The shared buffer now contains the system call data, and Falco can access it directly through *libscap* (introduced in Chapter 3). No data is copied during this phase, which minimizes CPU utilization while optimizing cache coherency.

There are a few things to keep in mind with regard to system call capture in Falco. The first one is that the way system calls are packed in the buffer is flexible and doesn't necessarily reflect the arguments of the original calls. In some cases, the driver skips unneeded arguments to maximize performance. In other cases, the driver adds

---

2 For more information, see the article "Using the Linux Kernel Tracepoints" (*https://oreil.ly/5ulP5*) by Mathieu Desnoyer.

fields that contain state, useful context, or additional information. For example, a clone event in Falco contains many fields that add information about the newly created process, like the environment variables.

The second thing to keep in mind is that, even if system calls are by far the most important sources of data that the drivers capture, they are not the only ones. Using tracepoints, the drivers hook into other places in the kernel, like the scheduler, to capture context switches and signal deliveries. Take a look at this command:

```
$ sysdig evt.type=switch
```

This line of code displays events captured through the context switch tracepoint.

Which Driver Should You Use?

If you're not sure which driver you should use, here are some simple guidelines:

- Use the kernel module when you have an I/O-intensive workload and you care about keeping the instrumentation overhead as low as possible. The kernel module has lower overhead than the eBPF probe, and on machines that generate a high number of system calls it will have less of a performance impact on running processes. It's not easy to estimate how much better the kernel module will perform, since this depends on how many system calls a process is making, but expect the difference to be noticeable with disk- or network-intensive workloads that generate many system calls every second.

- You should also use the kernel module when you need to support a kernel older than Linux version 4.12.

- Use the eBPF probe in all other situations.

That's it!

Capturing System Calls Within Containers

The beauty of tracepoint-based kernel-level capture is that it sees everything that runs in a machine, inside or outside a container. Nothing escapes it. It is also easy to deploy, with no need to run anything inside the monitored containers, and it doesn't require sidecars.

Figure 4-5 shows how you deploy Falco in a containerized environment, with a simplified diagram of a machine running three containers (labeled 1, 2, and 3) based on different container runtimes.

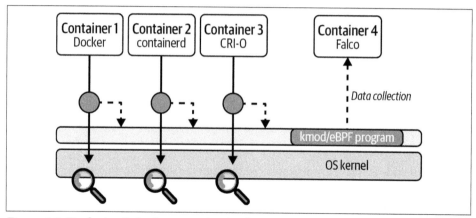

Figure 4-5. Deploying Falco in a containerized environment

In such a scenario, Falco is typically installed as a container. Orchestrators like Kubernetes make it easy to deploy Falco on every host, with facilities like DaemonSets and Helm charts.

When the Falco container starts, it installs the driver in the operating system. Once installed, the driver can see the system calls of any process in any container, with no further user action required, because all of these system calls go through the same tracepoint. Advanced logic in the driver can attribute each captured system call to its container so that Falco always knows which container has generated a system call. Falco also fetches metadata from the container runtime, making it easy to create rules that rely on container labels, image names, and other metadata. (Falco includes a further level of enrichment based on Kubernetes metadata, which we'll discuss in the next chapter.)

Running the Falco Drivers

Now that you have an idea of how they work, let's take a look at how to deploy and use the two Falco drivers on a local machine. (If you want to install Falco in production environments, see Chapters 9 and 10.)

Kernel Module

Falco, by default, runs using the kernel module, so no additional steps are required if you want to use that as your driver. Just run Falco, and it will pick up the kernel module. If you want to unload the kernel module and load a different version, for example because you have built your own customized module, use the following commands:

```
$ sudo rmmod falco
$ sudo insmod path/to/your/module/falco.ko
```

eBPF Probe

To enable eBPF support in Falco, you need to set the `FALCO_BPF_PROBE` environment variable. If you set it to an empty value (`FALCO_BPF_PROBE=""`), Falco will load the eBPF probe from *~/.falco/falco-bpf.o*. Otherwise, you can explicitly point to the path where the eBPF probe resides:

```
export FALCO_BPF_PROBE="path/to/your/ebpf/probe/falco-bpf.o"
```

After setting the environment variable, just run Falco normally and it will use the eBPF probe.

> To ensure that Falco's eBPF probe (and any other eBPF program) runs with the best performance, make sure that your kernel has `CONFIG_BPF_JIT` enabled and that `net.core.bpf_jit_enable` is set to 1. This enables the BPF JIT compiler in the kernel, substantially speeding up the execution of eBPF programs.

Using Falco in Environments Where Kernel Access Is Not Available: pdig

Kernel instrumentation, whenever possible, is always the way to go. But what if you want to run Falco in environments where access to the kernel is not allowed? This is common in managed container environments, like AWS Fargate. In such environments, installing a kernel module is not an option because the cloud provider blocks it.

For these situations, the Falco developers have implemented a user-level instrumentation driver called *pdig* (*https://oreil.ly/amRqP*). It is built on top of ptrace, so it uses the same approach as strace. Like strace, pdig can operate in two ways: it can run a program that you specify on the command line, or it can attach to a running process. Either way, pdig instruments the process and its children in a way that produces a Falco-compatible stream of events.

Note that pdig, like strace, requires you to enable `CAP_SYS_PTRACE` for the container runtime. Make sure you launch your container with this capability, or pdig will fail.

The eBPF probe and kernel module work at the global host level, whereas pdig works at the process level. This can make container instrumentation more challenging. Fortunately, pdig can track the children of an instrumented process. This means that running the entrypoint of a container with pdig will allow you to capture every system call generated by any process for that container.

The biggest limitation of pdig is performance. ptrace is versatile, but it introduces substantial overhead on the instrumented processes. pdig employs several tricks to reduce this overhead, but it's still substantially slower than the kernel-level Falco drivers.

Running Falco with pdig

You run pdig with the path (and arguments, if any) of the process you want to trace, much as you would with strace. Here's an example:

```
$ pdig [-a] curl https://example.com/
```

The -a option enables the full filter, which provides a richer set of instrumented system calls. You probably don't want to use this option with Falco, for performance reasons.

You can also attach to a running process with the -p option:

```
$ pdig [-a] -p 1234
```

To observe any effect, you will need to have Falco running in a separate process. Use the -u command-line flag:

```
$ falco -u
```

This will enable user-space instrumentation.

Falco Plugins

In addition to system calls, Falco can collect and process many other types of data, such as application logs and cloud activity streams. Let's round out this chapter by exploring the mechanism at the base of this functionality: Falco's plugins framework.

Plugins are a modular, flexible way to extend Falco ingestion. Anyone can use them to add a new source of data, local or remote, to Falco. Figure 4-6 indicates where plugins sit in the Falco capture stack: they are inputs for *libscap* and act as alternatives to the drivers that are used when capturing system calls.

Plugins are implemented as shared libraries that conform to a documented API. They allow you to add new event sources that you can then evaluate using filtering expressions and Falco rules. They also let you define new fields that can extract information from events.

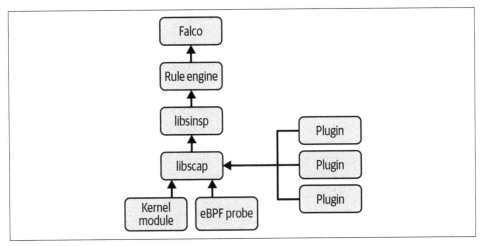

Figure 4-6. Falco plugins

Plugin Architecture Concepts

Plugins are dynamic shared libraries (*.so* files in Unix, *.dll* files in Windows) that export C calling convention functions. Falco dynamically loads these libraries and calls the exported functions. Plugins are versioned using semantic versioning to minimize regressions and compatibility issues. They can be written in any language, as long as they export the required functions. Go is the preferred language for writing plugins, followed by C/C++.

Plugins include two main pieces of functionality, also called *capabilities*:

Event sourcing

This capability is used to implement a new event source. An event source can "open" and "close" a stream of events and can return an event to *libscap* via a `next` method. In other words, it's used to feed new "stuff" to Falco.

Field extraction

Field extraction focuses on producing fields from events generated by other plugins or by the core libraries. Fields, you'll recall, are the basic components of Falco rules, so exposing new fields is equivalent to expanding the applicability of Falco rules to new domains. An example is JSON parsing, where a plugin might be able to extract fields from arbitrary JSON payloads. You'll learn more about fields in Chapter 6.

An individual plugin can offer the event sourcing capability, field extraction capability, or both at the same time. Capabilities are exported by implementing certain functions in the plugin API interface.

To make it easier to write plugins, there are Go (*https://oreil.ly/ylcdv*) and C++ (*https://oreil.ly/0c2CH*) SDKs that handle the details of memory management and type conversion. They provide a streamlined way to implement plugins without having to deal with all the details of lower-level functions that make up the plugin API.

The libraries will do everything possible to validate data that comes from the plugins, to protect Falco and other consumers from corrupted data. However, for performance reasons plugins are trusted, and because they run in the same thread and address space as Falco, they *could* crash the program. Falco assumes that you, as a user, are in control and will make sure only plugins you have vetted are loaded or packaged.

How Falco Uses Plugins

Falco loads plugins based on the configuration in *falco.yaml*. As of summer 2022, when this book went to press, if a source plugin is loaded, the only events processed are from that plugin, and system call capture is disabled. Also, a running Falco instance can use only one plugin. If, on a single machine, you want Falco to collect data from multiple plugins or from plugins and drivers, you will need to run multiple Falco instances and use a different source for each of them.[3]

Falco configures plugins via the `plugins` property in *falco.yaml*. Here's an example:

```
plugins:
  - name: cloudtrail
    library_path: libcloudtrail.so
    init_config: "..."
    open_params: "..."

load_plugins: [cloudtrail]
```

The `plugins` property in *falco.yaml* defines the set of plugins that Falco can load, and the `load_plugins` property controls which plugins load when Falco starts.

The mechanics of loading a plugin are implemented in *libscap* and leverage the dynamic library functionality of the operating system.[4] The plugin loading code also ensures that:

- The plugin is valid (i.e., it exports the set of expected symbols).
- The plugin's API version number is compatible with the plugin framework.

---

3 Note that the Falco developers are working on removing this limitation. As a consequence, in the future Falco will be able to receive data from multiple plugins at the same time or to capture system calls and at the same time use plugins.

4 A dynamic library is loaded using `dlopen`/`dlsym` in Unix, or `LoadLibrary`/`GetProcAddress` in Windows.

- Only one source plugin is loaded at a time for a given event source.
- If a mix of source and extractor plugins is loaded for a given event source, the exported fields have unique names that don't overlap across plugins.

An up-to-date list of available Falco plugins can be found in the plugins repository (*https://oreil.ly/g495C*) under the Falcosecurity GitHub organization. As of this writing, the Falcosecurity organization officially maintains plugins for CloudTrail, GitHub, Okta, Kubernetes audit logs, and JSON. In addition to these, there are third-party plugins available for seccomp and Docker.

If you are interested in writing your own plugins, you will find everything you need to know in Chapter 14. If you're impatient and just want to get to the code, you can find the source code for all the currently available plugins in the plugins repo.

Conclusion

Congratulations on making it to the end of a rich chapter packed with a lot of information! What you learned here is at the core of understanding and operating Falco. It also constitutes a solid architectural foundation that will be useful every time you need to run or deploy a security tool on Linux.

Next, you're going to learn about how context is added to the captured data to make Falco even more powerful.

CHAPTER 5

Data Enrichment

Falco's architecture allows you to capture events from different data sources, as you've learned. This process delivers raw data, which can be very rich but isn't very useful for runtime security unless paired with the right context. That's why Falco first extracts and then enriches the raw data with contextual information, so that the rule author can comfortably use it. Typically, we refer to this information as the event *metadata*. Getting metadata can be a complex task, and getting it efficiently is even more complex.

You've already seen that the system-state collection capabilities in *libscap* and the state engine implemented by *libsinsp* (discussed in Chapter 3) are central to this activity, but there's much more to discover. In this chapter, we'll delve into the design aspects of the Falco stack to help you better understand how data enrichment works. In particular, we will show you *libsinsp*'s efficient layered approach to obtaining system, container, and Kubernetes metadata for system call (syscall) events. This is what enables you to access the information you need relating to different contexts (depending on your use case), such as a container's ID or the name of a Pod where a suspicious event occurred. Finally, we'll show you how plugins, Falco's other main data source, can implement their own data enrichment mechanisms, opening up infinite possibilities.

Understanding Data Enrichment for Syscalls

Understanding how data enrichment works will help you to fully understand Falco's mechanics. Moreover, although data enrichment usually works out of the box, each context Falco supports has its own implementation and may need a specific configuration. Knowing the implementation details will help you troubleshoot and fine-tune Falco.

Data enrichment in Falco refers to the process of providing the rule engine with event metadata obtained by decoding the raw data or collecting it from complementary sources. You can then use this metadata as fields in both rule conditions and output formatting. Falco organizes the collected metadata in a set of field classes, so you can easily recognize which context they belong to. (You can find the complete list of supported fields in Chapter 6 or, if you have a Falco installation at your fingertips, by typing `falco --list`.)

One of the most significant examples of data enrichment is when using system calls as a data source, which you learned about in Chapter 4. Since syscalls are essential to every application, they occur in just about every context. Information directly provided by a syscall would not be useful without context, however, so it therefore becomes critical to collect and connect the surrounding information.

Table 5-1 shows the different categories of metadata that Falco collects for syscalls, and the field classes associated with each data enrichment layer.

Table 5-1. Contextual metadata for system calls

Context	Metadata	Field classes
Operating system	Processes and threads File descriptors Users and groups Network interfaces	`proc`, `thread`, `fd`, `fdlist`, `user`, `group`
Container	ID and name Type Image name Privileged Mount points Health checks	`container`
Kubernetes	Namespace Pod ReplicationController Service ReplicaSet Deployment	`k8s`

The enrichment process happens in user space and involves several components of Falco's stack. Most importantly, the metadata must be immediately available every time the rule engine requests it. Collecting it from other complementary sources on the fly would thus not be feasible, as attempting to do so would risk blocking the rule engine and the entire flow of incoming events.

For that reason, data enrichment involves two distinct phases. The first initializes a local state by collecting in bulk the data that is present when Falco starts, and the second continuously updates the local state while Falco runs. Having a local state allows Falco to extract metadata immediately. This design is shared among all implementation layers, as you will discover in the following sections.

Kubernetes Support and the Kubernetes Audit Log Data Source

In the Falco documentation, you will find mention of both Kubernetes support and Kubernetes Audit Events support (*https://oreil.ly/f565p*). You might think enabling Kubernetes support implies adding support for Kubernetes audit logs as a data source, but they're actually two distinct features.

Kubernetes support only concerns Falco's ability to enrich an event originating from a syscall with Kubernetes metadata. In rules, that metadata is available through the k8s field class. That's what we'll talk about in this chapter.

On the other hand, the Kubernetes audit log is an independent data source,[1] providing events that do not originate from a syscall. You can quickly identify rules that use this data source because they include source: k8s_audit. To use the Kubernetes audit log as a data source, you must enable support for audit logging in Kubernetes and use Falco's k8saudit plugin (*https://oreil.ly/p7OsC*); Kubernetes then directly feeds Falco with events, sending them via a webhook. The Kubernetes audit log data source already provides all the necessary context data along with the originating event, and therefore no specific enrichment mechanism is needed. The metadata is accessible through the ka field class.

You can enable the two features (support for Kubernetes and for the audit log as a data source) separately, since they are not dependent on each other.

Operating System Metadata

As you learned in Chapter 3, *libscap* and *libsinsp* work together to provide all the necessary infrastructure to create and update contextual information in a hierarchical structure composed of several state tables (see Figure 3-4 if you need a refresher). Those tables include information about:

- Processes and threads
- File descriptors
- Users and groups
- Network interfaces

---

1 In older Falco versions, the Kubernetes audit log was a built-in data source. From Falco 0.32, this data source has been refactored out as a plugin.

At a high level, the mechanism for collecting system information is relatively simple. At start time, one of *libscap*'s tasks is to scan the *process information pseudo-filesystem* (*https://oreil.ly/xso1E*), or *procfs*, which provides a user-space interface to the Linux kernel data structures and contains most of the information to initialize the state tables. It also collects system information (not available in */proc*) using functions provided by the standard C library, which in turn obtains the data from the underlying operating system (for example, `getpwent` and `getgrent` for users and groups lists, respectively, and `getifaddrs` for the network interfaces list). At this point, the initialization phase is complete.

libscap and *libsinsp* rely on the host's procfs to access the host's system information. That happens by default when Falco runs on the host since it can directly access the host's */proc*. However, when Falco runs in a container, the */proc* inside the container refers to a different namespace. In such a situation, you can configure *libscap* via the `HOST_ROOT` environment variable to read from an alternative path. If you set `HOST_ROOT`, *libscap* will use its value as a base path when looking for system paths. For example, when running Falco in a container, the usual approach is to mount the host's */proc* to */host/proc* inside the container and set `HOST_ROOT` to */host*. With this setup, *libscap* will read from */host/proc*, and thus it will use the information provided by the host's procfs.

Afterward, *libsinsp* comes into play with its state engine (see Figure 5-1). It updates the tables by inspecting the constantly captured stream of syscalls provided by the driver, which runs in kernel space. After the initialization phase, Falco will not need to make any syscalls or tap into the system to obtain updates from the Linux kernel. This approach has the double benefit of not creating noise in the system and having a low impact on performance. Furthermore, this technique enables *libsinsp* to discover system changes with low latency, allowing Falco to function as a streaming engine (one of its most important design goals).

The last important thing to note is that *libsinsp* updates the state tables before dispatching the event to the rule engine. This ensures that when the conditions or output require metadata, it will always be available and consistent. You can then find the system metadata grouped in the set of field classes you saw in Table 5-1: `proc`, `thread`, `fd`, `fdlist`, `user`, and `group`.

This set of information represents the basic metadata that enables a rule author to make a syscall event usable. Think about it: how would you use a numeric file descriptor in a rule? A filename is much better!

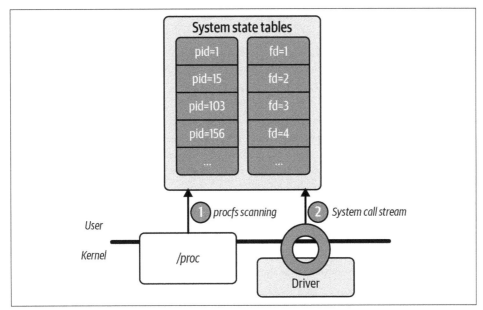

Figure 5-1. System state collection before (1) and after (2) the initialization phase

The system information (i.e., the state tables) produced by this data enrichment layer is also essential for collecting contextual information at the container level. We'll look at that next.

Container Metadata

Additional fundamental contextual information resides in the container runtime layer. A *container runtime* is a software component that can run containers on a host operating system. It is commonly responsible for managing container images and the lifecycles of containers running on your system. It is also responsible for managing a set of information related to each running container and providing that information to other applications.

Because Falco is a cloud native runtime security tool, it needs to be able to deal with container information. To achieve this goal, *libsinsp* works with the most commonly used container runtime environments, including Docker, Podman, and CRI-compatible[2] runtimes like containerd and CRI-O.

When *libsinsp* finds a running container runtime on the host, the container metadata enrichment functionality works out of the box in almost all cases. For example,

---

2 The Container Runtime Interface (CRI) (*https://oreil.ly/fiCGp*) is a plugin interface introduced by Kubernetes that enables the kubelet to use any container runtimes implementing the CRI.

libsinsp tries to use Docker's Unix socket at */var/run/docker.sock*; if this exists, *libsinsp* automatically connects to it and starts grabbing container metadata. *libsinsp* does the same for Podman and containerd. For other CRI-compatible runtimes, you will need to pass the socket path to Falco using the `--cri` command-line flag (for CRI-O, for example, you would pass `/var/run/crio/crio.sock`).

If the `HOST_ROOT` environment variable is set, *libsinsp* will use its value as the base path when looking for those Unix sockets. For example, when running Falco in a container, it's common to set `HOST_ROOT=/host` and mount */var/run/docker.sock* to */host/var/run/docker.sock* inside the container.

Regardless of which container runtime you are using, at initialization *libsinsp* requests a list of all running containers, which it uses to initialize an internal cache. At the same time, *libsinsp* updates the state table of running processes and threads, associating each of them with its respective container ID, if any.

libsinsp handles subsequent updates by using the syscalls stream coming from the driver (similar to what it does for system information). Since container information is always associated with a process, *libsinsp* tracks all new processes and threads. When it detects one, it looks up the corresponding container ID in the internal cache. If the container ID is not in the cache, *libsinsp* queries the container runtime to gather the missing data.

Dealing with Missing Metadata

The process of querying the container runtime happens asynchronously to avoid blocking the stream of events. In some environments, this operation is not fast enough to be completed asynchronously, so attempting it leads to empty container metadata fields. For CRI-compatible runtimes, Falco provides an option to disable asynchronous metadata fetching:

```
--disable-cri-async
```

Although you won't generally need to use this, it can be helpful if you need to wait for all the container metadata to be fetched before moving to the next input event so that no metadata is lost. However, you might see a performance penalty depending on the number of containers and the frequency with which they are created, started, and stopped. Disabling asynchronous fetching can be helpful when debugging or in systems with a very low syscall rate. In other circumstances, performance may be significantly degraded.

Ultimately, each syscall-generated event that occurs in a container has a process or thread ID that maps to a container ID and, consequently, to the container metadata (as shown in Figure 5-2). So, when the rule engine requires this metadata, *libsinsp* looks it up from the state tables and returns system information along with the container metadata. You will find the available container metadata grouped in the field class `container`, which can be used in both conditions and output formatting.

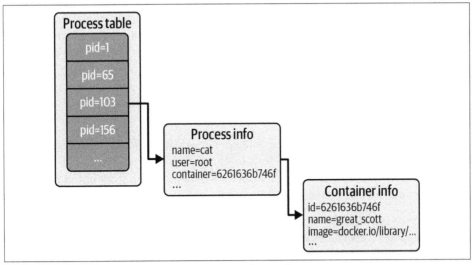

Figure 5-2. Container info in the libsinsp state hierarchy

Note that the field `container.id` can contain either the container ID *or* the special value `host`. This special value indicates that the event did not happen inside a container. The condition `container.id != host` is a common way to express a rule that applies only in the context of a container.

In the final data enrichment layer, Falco collects the Kubernetes metadata associated with system calls. We'll look at how this works next.

Kubernetes Metadata

Kubernetes, the flagship project of the Cloud Native Computing Foundation, is an open source platform for managing workloads and services. It has introduced many new concepts that make it easier to manage and scale clusters and is the most popular container orchestration system today.

One of the essential features of Kubernetes is encapsulating your applications in objects called *Pods*, which contain one or more containers. Pods are ephemeral objects that you can quickly deploy and easily replicate. *Services* in Kubernetes are an abstraction that allows you to expose a set of Pods as a single network service. Finally, Kubernetes lets you arrange those and many other objects into *namespaces*, which are objects that allow partitioning of a single cluster into multiple virtual clusters.

While these concepts greatly facilitate managing and automating clusters, they also introduce a set of contextual information about how and where your application is running. Awareness of this information is essential, since knowing that something has happened in your Kubernetes cluster is of little use if you don't know where it happened (for example, in which namespace or Pod). Falco collects information such as the container image name, Pod name, namespace, labels, annotations, and exposed service names so it can offer as accurate a view as possible of your deployments and applications. This is important for runtime alerting and protection of your infrastructure, because you're typically much more interested in what service or deployment is showing a strange behavior than in getting a container ID or some other hard-to-link piece of information. As a cloud native tool, Falco can readily obtain this metadata and attach it to the event.

Similar to the operating system and container metadata collection mechanisms you saw in the previous sections, this feature allows Falco to enrich syscall events by adding Kubernetes metadata. For full Kubernetes support, you must opt in by passing two command-line options to Falco:

`--k8s-api` *(or just `-k`)*
    This enables Kubernetes support by connecting to the API server specified as an argument (e.g., `http://admin:password@127.0.0.1:8080`).

`--k8s-api-cert` *(or just `-K`)*
    This provides certificate materials to authenticate the user and (optionally) verify the Kubernetes API server's identity.

Further details are provided in Chapter 10.

When Falco is running in a Pod, Kubernetes injects that information in the container, so you just need to set:

    -k https://$(KUBERNETES_SERVICE_HOST)
    -K /var/run/secrets/kubernetes.io/serviceaccount/token

Most installation methods use this strategy to fetch those values automatically.

Once Kubernetes support is configured, *libsinsp* will get all the necessary data from Kubernetes to create and maintain a local copy of the state of the cluster. However, unlike the other enrichment mechanisms that get metadata locally from the host, *libsinsp* has to connect to the Kubernetes API server (usually a remote endpoint) to get cluster information. Because of this difference, the implementation design needs to take performance and scalability concerns into account.

A typical Falco deployment (pictured in Figure 5-3) runs one Falco sensor on every node in the cluster. At startup, each sensor connects to the API server to collect the cluster data and build the initial state locally. From then on, each sensor will use the Kubernetes watch API (*https://oreil.ly/g0hCZ*) to periodically update the local state.

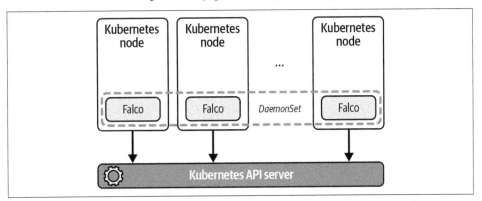

Figure 5-3. A Falco deployment using a DaemonSet (https://oreil.ly/WTTGU) to ensure that all nodes run a copy of a Pod

Since Falco sensors are distributed in the cluster (one per node) and grab data from the API server—and because collecting some resource types from Kubernetes may result in huge responses that severely impact both the API server and Falco—*libsinsp* has mechanisms to avoid congestion. First, it waits for a short time between downloading each chunk. Falco allows you to fine-tune that wait time, along with several other parameters, by changing a value in */etc/falco/falco.yaml*.

More importantly, it's possible to request *only* the relevant metadata for the targeted node from the API server. This is helpful because Falco's architecture is distributed, so each sensor needs data only from the node on which the event occurred. This optimization is fundamental if you want to scale Falco on a cluster with thousands of nodes. To enable it, add the --k8s-node flag to the Falco command-line arguments, passing the current node name as the value. You can usually obtain this name easily from the Kubernetes Downward API (*https://oreil.ly/F1Dnv*).[3]

If you don't include the --k8s-node flag, *libsinsp* will still be able to get the data from Kubernetes, but each Falco sensor will have to request the whole cluster's data. This can introduce a performance penalty on large clusters, so we strongly discourage it. (You will learn more about running Falco on a production Kubernetes cluster in Part III.)

---

3 The Downward API allows containers to consume information about themselves or the cluster without using the Kubernetes API server. Among other things, it allows exposing the current node name through an environment variable that can be then used in Falco command-line arguments.

An Alternative Way to Acquire Kubernetes Metadata

Although the method described in this section is the recommended way to obtain Kubernetes metadata, there's another, leaner working mode worth mentioning. *libsinsp* is smart enough to get a subset of the metadata even without connecting to the Kubernetes API server. That's possible because the kubelet (*https://oreil.ly/sUOMa*) annotates some metadata directly on the container: specifically the ID, name, namespace, and labels of the Pod (which are usually the most relevant context information). Since *libsinsp* retrieves those annotations using the container runtime API, it also tries to use them when possible and falls back to the Kubernetes API server when the missing data is needed. This strategy is always enabled, so you won't need to configure it.

You can think of this as an optimization, but also as a feature. If the immediately available metadata is enough for your use case (for example, if you're using a custom ruleset that doesn't need the complete set of Kubernetes metadata), you don't have to enable full support for Kubernetes. If you don't, you will still get the ID, name, namespace, and labels of the Pod.

When Kubernetes metadata is available, you will find it grouped in the k8s field class. Many of the Falco default rules include k8s fields in their conditions. Falco, when used with the -pk command-line option, automatically appends the most crucial Kubernetes metadata to the output of all notifications, as you can see in the following example, which we've pretty-printed to improve readability (more on this in "Output Settings" on page 137):

```
15:29:40.515013896: Notice System user ran an interactive command
        (user=bin user_loginuid=-1 command=login container_id=46c99eea62a8
        image=docker.io/library/nginx)
        k8s.ns=default k8s.pod=my-app-84d64cb8fb-zmxgz
        container=46c99eea62a8
```

This output is the result of the complex mechanism you've just learned about that allows you to obtain accurate and contextualized information to immediately identify what event has just occurred, and where.

So far, we've only discussed Falco's data enrichment process for system calls. Although that's likely to be the most relevant information for most users, you should know that Falco also offers custom enrichment mechanisms. We'll take a quick look at how to implement those next.

Data Enrichment with Plugins

Plugins can extend Falco by adding new data sources and defining new fields to describe how to use these new events. As you'll recall from Chapter 4, a plugin that offers the field extraction capability works on events provided by other plugins or core libraries. While it might not seem obvious yet, a plugin with this capability has everything it takes to provide a custom data-enrichment mechanism. First, it can receive data from any data source. Second, it can define new fields. Fundamentally, it allows the plugin author to implement logic to return the values of those fields, thus potentially providing additional metadata. This opens the door to the possibility of implementing custom data enrichment.

When such a plugin runs, *libsinsp* calls the plugin function for field extraction for each incoming event. The function receives the raw payload of the event and the list of fields the rule engine needs. The plugin API interface does not impose any other constraints to make the extraction process work. Although data enrichment is possible in the flow just described, the plugin author will still have to consider all the implications of the use case; for example, the plugin will need to manage the local state and subsequent updates. Extracting fields and enriching the event is thus entirely up to the plugin author. The APIs merely provide the essential tools.

Chapter 14 shows you how to implement a plugin. If you're interested in doing that, however, our advice is to read the next chapter about fields and filters first, so you have a more complete picture of how extracting data works.

Conclusion

This chapter illustrated how Falco works internally to provide a rich set of metadata. Falco makes this metadata available as fields you can use in rules' conditions. Read on to discover how to use fields to filter only those events that are really pertinent to your needs.

CHAPTER 6

Fields and Filters

It's finally time to take all the theory you learned in the previous chapters and start putting it into practice. In this chapter you will learn about Falco filters: what they are, how they work, and how to use them.

Filters are at the core of Falco. They are also a powerful investigation instrument that can be used in several other tools, such as sysdig. As a consequence, we expect that you will come back and consult this chapter often, even after finishing the book—so we've structured it to be used as a reference. For example, it contains tables with all of the operators and data types the filtering language provides, designed for quick consultation, as well as a well-documented list of Falco's most useful fields. This chapter's contents will be handy pretty much every time you write a Falco rule, so make sure to bookmark it!

What Is a Filter?

Let's start with a semiformal definition:

> A *filter* in Falco is a condition containing a sequence of comparisons that are connected by Boolean operators. Each of the comparisons evaluates a field, which is extracted from an input event, against a constant, using a relational operator. Comparisons in filters are evaluated left to right, but parentheses can be used to define precedence. A filter is applied to an input event and returns a Boolean result indicating if the event matches the filter.

Ouch. That description is extremely dry and somewhat complicated. But if we unpack it, with the aid of some examples, you'll see it's not too bad. Let's start with the first sentence:

> A *filter* in Falco is a condition containing a sequence of comparisons that are connected by Boolean operators.

This just means that a filter looks like this:

```
A = B and not C != D
```

In other words, if you can write an `if` condition in any programming language, the filter syntax will look very familiar. Here's the next sentence:

> Each of the comparisons evaluates a field, which is extracted from an input event, against a constant, using a relational operator.

This tells us that Falco's filtering syntax is based on the concept of *fields*, which we will describe in detail later in this chapter. Field names have a dotted syntax and appear on the left side of each comparison. On the right side is a constant value that will be compared against the field. Here's an example:

```
proc.name = emacs or proc.pid != 1234
```

Moving on:

> Comparisons in filters are evaluated left to right, but parentheses can be used to define precedence.

This means you can organize your filter using parentheses. For example:

```
proc.name = emacs or (proc.name = vi and container.name=redis)
```

Again, this works exactly the same as using parentheses inside a logical expression in your favorite programming language. Now for the final sentence:

> A filter is applied to an input event and returns a Boolean result indicating if the event matches the filter.

When you specify a filter in a Falco rule, the filter is applied to every input event. For example, if you're using one of Falco's drivers, filters are applied to every system call. The filter evaluates the system call and returns a Boolean value: `true` or `false`. `true` means that the event satisfies the filter (we say that the filter *matches* the event), while `false` means that the filter rejects, or drops, the event. For example, this filter:

```
proc.name = emacs or proc.name = vi
```

matches (returns `true` for) every system call generated by processes called `emacs` or `vi`.

That's essentially all you need to know at a high level. Now let's dive into the details.

Filtering Syntax Reference

From a syntactical point of view, as we mentioned, writing a Falco filter is very similar to writing an `if` condition in any programming language, so if you have basic programming experience, you shouldn't expect any major surprises. However, there are some areas that are specific to the type of matching you do in Falco. This section takes a look at the syntax in detail, giving you the full picture.

Relational Operators

Table 6-1 provides a reference of all of the available relational operators, including an example for each of them.

Table 6-1. Falco's relational operators

Operator	Description	Example
=, !=	General equality/inequality operators. Can be used with all types of fields.	`proc.name = emacs`
<=, <, >=, >	Numeric comparison operators. Can be used with numeric fields only.	`evt.buflen > 100`
contains	Can be used with string fields only. Performs a case-sensitive string search for the given constant inside the field value, and returns `true` if the field value contains the constant.	`fd.filename contains passwd`
icontains	Like `contains`, but case-insensitive.	`user.name icontains john`
bcontains	Like `contains`, but allows you to perform checks on binary buffers.	`evt.buf bcontains DEADBEEF`
startswith	Can be used with string fields only. Returns `true` if the given constant matches the beginning of the field value.	`fd.directory startswith "/etc"`
bstartswith	Like `startswith`, but allows you to perform checks on binary buffers.	`evt.buf bstartswith DEADBEEF`
endswith	Can be used with string fields only. Returns `true` if the given constant matches the end of the field value.	`fd.filename endswidth ".key"`
in	Compares the field value to multiple constants and returns `true` if one or more of those constants equals the field value. Can be used with all fields, including numeric fields and string fields.	`proc.name in (vi, emacs)`
intersects	Returns `true` when a field with multiple values includes at least one value that matches one of the provided constants.	`ka.req.pod.volumes.host path intersects (/proc, /var/run/docker.sock)`
pmatch	Returns `true` if one of the constants is a prefix of the field value. Note: pmatch can be used as an alternative to the `in` operator, and performs better with large sets of constants because it is implemented internally as a trie instead of multiple comparisons.	`fd.name pmatch (/var/run, /etc, /lib, /usr/lib)` `fd.name = /var/run/docker` succeeds because `/var/run` is a prefix of `/var/run/docker`. `fd.name = /boot` does not succeed because no constant is a prefix of `/boot`. `fd.name = /var` does not succeed because no constant is a prefix of `/var`.
exists	Returns `true` if the given field exists for the input event.	`evt.res exists`

Operator	Description	Example
glob	Matches the given string against the field value according to Unix shell wildcard patterns. For more details, enter `man 7 glob` in your terminal.	`fd.name glob '/home/*/.ssh/*'`

Logical Operators

The logical operators that you can use in Falco filters are straightforward and don't include any surprises. Table 6-2 lists them and provides examples.

Table 6-2. Falco's logical operators

Operator	Example
and	`proc.name = emacs and proc.cmdline contains myfile.txt`
or	`proc.name = emacs or proc.name = vi`
not	`not proc.name = emacs`

Strings and Quoting

String constants can be specified without quotation marks:

```
proc.name = emacs
```

Quotes can, however, be used to enclose strings that include spaces or special characters. Both single quotes and double quotes are accepted. For example:

```
proc.name = "my process" or proc.name = 'my process'
```

This means you can include quotes in strings:

```
evt.buffer contains '"'
```

Fields

As you can see, Falco filters are not very complicated. However, they are extremely flexible and powerful. This power comes from the fields you can use in filtering conditions. Falco gives you access to a variety of fields, each of which exposes a property of the input events that Falco captures. Since fields are so important, let's take a look at how they work and how they are organized. Then we'll discuss which ones to use and when.

Argument Fields Versus Enrichment Fields

Fields expose properties of input events as typed values. A field, for example, can be a string, like the process name, or a number, like the process ID.

At the highest level, Falco offers two categories of fields. The first category includes the fields that are obtained by dissecting input events. System call arguments, like the filename for an open system call or the buffer argument for a read system call, are examples of such fields. You access these fields with the following syntax, where *X* is the name of the argument you want to access:

```
evt.arg.X
```

or, where *N* is the position of the argument:

```
evt.arg[N]
```

For example:

```
evt.arg.name = /etc/passwd
evt.arg[1] = /etc/passwd
```

To find out which arguments a specific event type supports, sysdig is your friend. The output line for an event in sysdig will show you all of its arguments and their names.

The second category consists of fields that derive from the enrichment process that *libsinsp* performs while capturing system calls and other events, described in Chapter 5. Falco exports many fields that expose the content of *libsinsp*'s thread and file descriptor tables, adding rich context about the events received from the drivers.

To help you understand how this works, let's take the proc.cwd field as an example. For each system call that Falco captures, this field contains the current working directory of the process that issued the system call. This is handy if you want to capture all of the system calls generated by processes that are currently running inside a specific directory; for example:

```
proc.cwd = /tmp
```

The working directory of the process is not part of the system call, so exposing this field requires tracking the working directory of a process and attaching it to every system call that the process generates. This, in turn, involves four steps:

1. Collect the working directory when a process starts, and store it in the process's entry in the thread table.

2. Keep track of when the process changes its working directory (by intercepting and parsing the chdir system call), and update the thread table entry accordingly.

3. Resolve the thread ID of every system call to identify the corresponding thread table entry.

4. Return the thread table entry's cwd value.

libsinsp does all of this, which means that the proc.cwd field is available for every system call, not only for directory-related ones like chdir. It's impressive how much hard work Falco does to expose this field to you!

Enrichment-based filtering is powerful because it allows you to filter system calls (and any other events) based on properties that are not included with the syscalls themselves, but are of great use for security policies. For example, the following filter allows you to capture the system calls that read from or write to */etc/passwd*:

```
evt.is_io=true and fd.name=/etc/passwd
```

It works even if these system calls originally don't contain any information about the filename (they operate on file descriptors). The hundreds of enrichment-based fields available out of the box are the main reason why Falco is so powerful and versatile.

Mandatory Fields Versus Optional Fields

Some fields exist for every input event, and you will be guaranteed to find them regardless of the event type or family. Examples of such fields are `evt.ts`, `evt.dir`, and `evt.type`.

However, most fields are optional and only present in some input event types. Typically, you don't have to worry about this, as fields that don't exist will just evaluate to `false` without generating an error. For example, the following check will evaluate to `false` for all events that don't have an argument called `name`:

```
evt.arg.name contains /etc
```

In some cases, though, you might want to explicitly check if a field exists. One reason would be to resolve ambiguities like whether the filter `evt.arg.name != /etc` returns `true` or `false` for events that don't have an argument called `name`. You can answer questions like this by using the `exists` relational operator:

```
evt.arg.name exists and evt.arg.name != /etc
```

Field Types

Fields have types, which are used to validate values and ensure the syntactic correctness of filters. Take the following filter:

```
proc.pid = hello
```

Falco and sysdig will reject this with the following error:

```
filter error at position 16: hello is not a valid number
```

This happens because the `proc.pid` field is of type `INT64`, so its value must be an integer. The typing system also allows Falco to improve the rendering of some fields by understanding the meaning behind them. For example, `evt.arg.res` is of type `ERRNO`, which by default is a number. However, when possible, Falco will resolve it into an error code string (such as `EAGAIN`), which improves the readability and usability of the field.

When we looked at relational operators, we noted how some are very similar to the ones in most programming languages, while others are unique to Falco filters. The same is true for field types. Table 6-3 lists the types you may encounter in Falco filter fields.

Table 6-3. Field types

Type	Description
INT8, INT16, INT32, INT64, UINT8, UINT16, UINT32, UINT64, DOUBLE	Numeric types, like in your favorite programming language.
CHARBUF	A printable buffer of characters.
BYTEBUF	A raw buffer of bytes not suitable for printing.
ERRNO	An INT64 value that, when possible, is resolved to an error code.
FD	An INT64 value that, when possible, is resolved to the value of the file descriptor. For example, for a file this gets resolved to the filename; for a socket it gets resolved to the TCP connection tuple.
PID	An INT64 value that, when possible, is resolved to the process name.
FSPATH	A string containing a relative or absolute filesystem path.
SYSCALLID	A 16-bit system call ID. When possible, the value gets resolved to the system call name.
SIGTYPE	An 8-bit signal number that, when possible, gets resolved to the signal name (e.g., SIGCHLD).
RELTIME	A relative time, with nanosecond precision, rendered as a human-readable string.
ABSTIME	An absolute time interval.
PORT	A TCP/UDP port. When possible, this gets resolved to a protocol name.
L4PROTO	A 1-byte IP protocol type. When possible, this gets resolved to a L4 protocol name (TCP, UDP).
BOOL	A Boolean value.
IPV4ADDR	An IPv4 address.
DYNAMIC	An indication that the field type can vary depending on the context. Used for generic fields like evt.rawarg.
FLAGS8, FLAGS16, FLAGS32	A flags word (i.e., a set of flags encoded as a number using binary encoding) that, when possible, is converted into a readable string (e.g., O_RDONLY|O_CLOEXEC). The resolution into the string is dependent on the context, as events can register their own flag values. So, for example, flags for an lseek system call event will be converted into values like SEEK_END, SEEK_CUR, and SEEK_SET, while sockopt flags will be converted into SOL_SOCKET, SOL_TCP, and so on.
UID	A Unix user ID, resolved to a username when possible.
GID	A Unix group ID, resolved to a group name when possible.
IPADDR	An IPv4 or IPv6 address.
IPNET	An IPv4 or IPv6 network.
MODE	A 32-bit bitmask to represent file modes.

How do you find out the type of a field you want to use? The best way is to invoke Falco with the --list and -v options:

```
$ falco --list -v
```

This will print the full list of fields, including type information for each entry in the list.

Using Fields and Filters

Now that you've learned about filters and fields, let's take a look at how you can use them in practice. We'll focus on Falco and sysdig.

Fields and Filters in Falco

Fields and filters are at the core of Falco rules. Fields are used to express rules' conditions and are part of both conditions and outputs. To demonstrate how, we'll craft our own rule.

Let's say we would like Falco to notify us every time there is an attempt to change the permissions of a file and make it executable by another user. When that happens, we would like to know the name of the file that was changed, the new mode of the file, and the name of the user who caused the trouble. We would also like to know whether the mode change attempt was successful or not.

Here is the rule:

```
- rule: File Becoming Executable by Others
  desc: Attempt to make a file executable by other users
  condition: >
    (evt.type=chmod or evt.type=fchmod or evt.type=fchmodat)
    and evt.arg.mode contains S_IXOTH
  output: >
    attempt to make a file executable by others
    (file=%evt.arg.filename mode=%evt.arg.mode user=%user.name
    failed=%evt.failed)
  priority: WARNING
```

The `condition` section is where the rule's filter is specified.

File modes, including the executable bit, are changed using the `chmod` system call, or one of its variants. Therefore, the first part of the filter selects events that are of type `chmod`, `fchmod`, or `fchmodat`:

```
evt.type=chmod or evt.type=fchmod or evt.type=fchmodat
```

Now that we have the right system calls, we want to accept only the subset of them that set the "other" executable bit. Reading the `chmod` manual page (*https://oreil.ly/zuKuC*) reveals that the flag we need to check is `S_IXOTH`. We determine its presence by using the `contains` operator:

```
evt.arg.mode contains S_IXOTH
```

Combining the two pieces with an and gives us the full filter. Easy!

Now, let's focus our attention on the output section of the rule. This is where we tell Falco what to print on the screen when the rule's condition returns true. You will notice that this is just a printf-like string that mixes regular text with fields, whose values will be resolved in the final message:

```
attempt to make a file executable by others (file=%evt.arg.filename
mode=%evt.arg.mode user=%user.name failed=%evt.failed)
```

The only thing you need to remember is that you need to prefix field names in the output string with the % character; otherwise, they will just be treated as part of the string.

Time for you to try this! Save the preceding rule in a file called *ch6.yaml*. After that, run this command line in a terminal:

```
$ sudo falco -r ch6.yaml
```

Then, in another terminal, run these two commands:

```
$ echo test > test.txt
$ chmod o+x test.txt
```

This is the output you will get in the Falco terminal:

```
17:26:43.796934201: Warning attempt to make a file executable by others
(file=/home/loris/test.txt mode=S_IXOTH|S_IWOTH|S_IROTH|S_IXGRP|S_IWGRP
|S_IRGRP|S_IXUSR|S_IWUSR|S_IRUSR user=root failed=false)
```

Congratulations, you've just performed your very own Falco detection! Note how evt.arg.mode and evt.failed are rendered in a human-readable way, even if internally they are numbers. This shows you the power of the filter/fields type system.

Fields and Filters in sysdig

An introduction to sysdig was provided in Chapter 4 (if you need a refresher, see "sysdig" on page 45). Here we will look specifically at how filters and fields are used in sysdig.

While Falco is based on the concepts of rules and of notifying the user when rules match, sysdig focuses on investigation, troubleshooting, and threat-hunting workflows. In sysdig, you use filters to *restrict* the input, and you (optionally) use field formatting to *control* the output. The combination of the two provides a ton of flexibility during investigations.

Filters in sysdig are specified at the end of the command line:

```
$ sudo sysdig proc.name=echo
```

Output formatting is provided using the -p command-line flag and uses the same printf-like syntax that we just described when talking about Falco outputs:

```
$ sudo sysdig -p"type:%evt.type proc:%proc.name" proc.name=echo
```

An important thing to keep in mind is that, when the -p flag is used, sysdig will only print an output line for the events in which *all* of the specified filters exist. So, this command:

```
$ sudo sysdig -p"%evt.res %proc.name"
```

will print a line only for events that have both a return value *and* a process name, skipping, for example, all the system call "enter" events. If you care about seeing all of the events, put a star (*) at the beginning of the formatting string:

```
$ sudo sysdig -p"*%evt.res %proc.name"
```

When a field is missing, it will be rendered as <NA>.

When no formatting is specified with -p, sysdig displays input events in a standard format that conveniently includes all of the arguments and argument names, for every system call. Here's an example sysdig output line for an openat system call, with the system call arguments highlighted in bold for visibility:

```
4831 20:50:01.473556825 2 cat (865.865) < openat fd=7(<f>/tmp/myfile.txt)
dirfd=-100(AT_FDCWD) name=/tmp/myfile.txt flags=1(O_RDONLY) mode=0 dev=4
```

Each of the arguments can be used in a filter with the evt.arg syntax:

```
$ sudo sysdig evt.arg.name=/tmp/myfile.txt
```

As a more advanced example, let's convert the *File Becoming Executable by Others* rule we created for Falco in the previous section into a sysdig command line:

```
$ sudo sysdig -p"attempt to make a file executable by others \
  (file=%evt.arg.filename mode=%evt.arg.mode user=%user.name \
  failed=%evt.failed)" \
  "(evt.type=chmod or evt.type=fchmod or evt.type=fchmodat) \
  and evt.arg.mode contains S_IXOTH"
```

This shows how easy it is to use sysdig as a development tool when creating new rules.

Falco's Most Useful Fields

This section presents a curated list of some of the most important Falco fields, organized by class. You can use this list as a reference when writing filters. For a full list, including all plugin fields, use the following at the command line:

```
$ falco --list -v
```

General

The fields listed in Table 6-4 apply to every event and include general properties of an event.

Table 6-4. evt filter class fields

Field name	Description
evt.num	The event number.
evt.time	The event timestamp as a string that includes the nanosecond part.
evt.dir	The event direction; can be either > for enter events or < for exit events.
evt.type	The name of the event (e.g., open).
evt.cpu	The number of the CPU where this event happened.
evt.args	All the event arguments, aggregated into a single string.
evt.rawarg	One of the event arguments, specified by name (e.g., evt.rawarg.fd).
evt.arg	One of the event arguments, specified by name or by number. Some events (such as return codes or file descriptors) will be converted into a text representation when possible (e.g., evt.arg.fd or evt.arg[0]).
evt.buffer	The binary data buffer for events that have one, like read, recvfrom, etc. Use this field in filters with contains to search in I/O data buffers.
evt.buflen	The length of the binary data buffer for events that have one, like read, recvfrom, etc.
evt.res	The event return value, as a string. If the event failed, the result is an error code string (e.g., ENOENT); otherwise, the result is the string SUCCESS.
evt.rawres	The event return value, as a number (e.g., -2). Useful for range comparisons.
evt.failed	true for events that returned an error status.

Processes

The fields in this class contain all the information you need about processes and threads. The information in Table 6-5 comes mostly from the process table that *libsinsp* constructs in memory.

Table 6-5. proc filter class fields

Field name	Description
proc.pid	The ID of the process generating the event.
proc.exe	The first command-line argument (usually the executable name or a custom one).
proc.name	The name (excluding the path) of the executable generating the event.
proc.args	The arguments passed on the command line when starting the process generating the event.
proc.env	The environment variables of the process generating the event.
proc.cwd	The current working directory of the event.
proc.ppid	The PID of the parent of the process generating the event.
proc.pname	The name (excluding the path) of the parent of the process generating the event.

Field name	Description
`proc.pcmdline`	The full command line (`proc.name` + `proc.args`) of the parent of the process generating the event.
`proc.logi nshellid`	The PID of the oldest shell among the ancestors of the current process, if there is one. This field can be used to separate different user sessions and is useful in conjunction with chisels like spy_user.
`thread.tid`	The ID of the thread generating the event.
`thread.vtid`	The ID of the thread generating the event as seen from its current PID namespace.
`proc.vpid`	The ID of the process generating the event as seen from its current PID namespace.
`proc.sid`	The session ID of the process generating the event.
`proc.sname`	The name of the current process's session leader. This is either the process with `pid=proc.sid` or the eldest ancestor that has the same session ID as the current process.
`proc.tty`	The controlling terminal of the process. This is 0 for processes without a terminal.

File Descriptors

Table 6-6 lists the fields related to file descriptors, which are at the base of I/O. Fields containing details about files and directories, network connections, pipes, and other types of interprocess communication can all be found in this class.

Table 6-6. fd filter class fields

Field name	Description
`fd.num`	The unique number identifying the file descriptor.
`fd.typechar`	The type of the file descriptor, as a single character. Can be f for file, 4 for IPv4 socket, 6 for IPv6 socket, u for Unix socket, p for pipe, e for eventfd, s for signalfd, l for eventpoll, i for inotify, or o for unknown.
`fd.name`	The full name of the file descriptor. If it's a file, this field contains the full path. If it's a socket, this field contains the connection tuple.
`fd.directory`	If the file descriptor is a file, the directory that contains it.
`fd.filename`	If the file descriptor is a file, the filename without the path.
`fd.ip`	*(Filter only)* Matches the IP address (client or server) of the file descriptor.
`fd.cip`	The client's IP address.
`fd.sip`	The server's IP address.
`fd.lip`	The local IP address.
`fd.rip`	The remote IP address.
`fd.port`	*(Filter only)* Matches the port (either client or server) of the file descriptor.
`fd.cport`	For TCP/UDP file descriptors, the client's port.
`fd.sport`	For TCP/UDP file descriptors, the server's port.
`fd.lport`	For TCP/UDP file descriptors, the local port.
`fd.rport`	For TCP/UDP file descriptors, the remote port.
`fd.l4proto`	The IP protocol of a socket. Can be tcp, udp, icmp, or raw.

Users and Groups

Table 6-7 lists the fields in the `user` and `group` filter classes.

Table 6-7. user and group filter class fields

Field name	Description
`user.uid`	The user's ID
`user.name`	The user's name
`group.gid`	The group's ID
`group.name`	The group's name

Containers

The fields in the `container` class (Table 6-8) can be used for everything related to containers, including obtaining IDs, names, labels, and mounts.

Table 6-8. container filter class fields

Field name	Description
`container.id`	The container ID.
`container.name`	The container name.
`container.image`	The container image name (e.g., `falcosecurity/falco:latest` for Docker).
`container.image.id`	The container image ID (e.g., `6f7e2741b66b`).
`container.privileged`	`true` for containers running as privileged, `false` otherwise.
`container.mounts`	A space-separated list of mount information. Each item in the list has the format *<source>*:*<dest>*:*<mode>*:*<rdrw>*:*<propagation>*.
`container.mount`	Information about a single mount, specified by number (e.g., `container.mount[0]`) or mount source (e.g., `container.mount[/usr/local]`). The pathname can be a glob (e.g., `container.mount[/usr/local/*]`), in which case the first matching mount will be returned. The information has the format *<source>*:*<dest>*:*<mode>*:*<rdrw>*:*<propagation>*. If there is no mount with the specified index or matching the provided source, this returns the string `"none"` instead of a NULL value.
`container.image.repository`	The container image repository (e.g., `falcosecurity/falco`).
`container.image.tag`	The container image tag (e.g., `stable`, `latest`).
`container.image.digest`	The container image registry digest (e.g., `sha256:d977378f890d445c15e51795296e4e5062f109ce6da83e0a355fc4ad8699d27`).

Kubernetes

When Falco is configured to interface with the Kubernetes API server, the fields in this class (listed in Table 6-9) can be used to fetch information about Kubernetes objects.

Table 6-9. k8s filter class fields

Field name	Description
k8s.pod.name	The Kubernetes Pod name.
k8s.pod.id	The Kubernetes Pod ID.
k8s.pod.label	The Kubernetes Pod label (e.g., k8s.pod.label.foo).
k8s.rc.name	The Kubernetes ReplicationController name.
k8s.rc.id	The Kubernetes ReplicationController ID.
k8s.rc.label	The Kubernetes ReplicationController label (e.g., k8s.rc.label.foo).
k8s.svc.name	The Kubernetes Service name. Can return more than one value, concatenated.
k8s.svc.id	The Kubernetes Service ID. Can return more than one value, concatenated.
k8s.svc.label	The Kubernetes Service label (e.g., k8s.svc.label.foo). Can return more than one value, concatenated.
k8s.ns.name	The Kubernetes namespace name.
k8s.ns.id	The Kubernetes namespace ID.
k8s.ns.label	The Kubernetes namespace label (e.g., k8s.ns.label.foo).
k8s.rs.name	The Kubernetes ReplicaSet name.
k8s.rs.id	The Kubernetes ReplicaSet ID.
k8s.rs.label	The Kubernetes ReplicaSet label (e.g., k8s.rs.label.foo).
k8s.deployment.name	The Kubernetes Deployment name.
k8s.deployment.id	The Kubernetes Deployment ID.
k8s.deployment.label	The Kubernetes Deployment label (e.g., k8s.rs.label.foo).

CloudTrail

The fields in the cloudtrail class (listed in Table 6-10) are available when the CloudTrail plugin is configured. They allow you to build filters and formatters for AWS detections.

Table 6-10. cloudtrail filter class fields

Field name	Description
ct.error	The error code from the event. Will be " " if there was no error.
ct.src	The source of the CloudTrail event (eventSource in the JSON).
ct.shortsrc	The source of the CloudTrail event (eventSource in the JSON), without the .amazonaws.com trailer.
ct.name	The name of the CloudTrail event (eventName in the JSON).

Field name	Description
ct.user	The user of the CloudTrail event (userIdentity.userName in the JSON).
ct.region	The region of the CloudTrail event (awsRegion in the JSON).
ct.srcip	The IP address generating the event (sourceIPAddress in the JSON).
ct.useragent	The user agent generating the event (userAgent in the JSON).
ct.readonly	true if the event only reads information (e.g., DescribeInstances), false if the event modifies the state (e.g., RunInstances, CreateLoadBalancer).
s3.uri	The S3 URI (s3://<bucket>/<key>).
s3.bucket	The bucket name for S3 events.
s3.key	The S3 key name.
ec2.name	The name of the EC2 instance, typically stored in the instance tags.

Kubernetes Audit Logs

Fields related to Kubernetes audit logs (listed in Table 6-11) are available when the k8saudit plugin is configured. The k8saudit plugin is responsible for interfacing Falco with the Kubernetes audit logs facility. The fields exported by the plugin can be used to monitor several types of Kubernetes activities.

Table 6-11. k8saudit filter class fields

Field name	Description
ka.user.name	The name of the user performing the request
ka.user.groups	The groups to which the user belongs
ka.verb	The action being performed
ka.uri	The request URI as sent from client to server
ka.uri.param	The value of a given query parameter in the URI (e.g., when uri=/foo? key=val, ka.uri.param[key] is val)
ka.target.name	The target object's name
ka.target.namespace	The target object's namespace
ka.target.resource	The target object's resource
ka.req.configmap.name	When the request object refers to a ConfigMap, the ConfigMap name
ka.req.pod.containers.image	When the request object refers to a Pod, the container's images
ka.req.pod.containers .privileged	When the request object refers to a Pod, the value of the privileged flag for all containers
ka.req.pod.containers .add_capabilities	When the request object refers to a Pod, all capabilities to add when running the container
ka.req.role.rules	When the request object refers to a role or cluster role, the rules associated with the role
ka.req.role.rules.verbs	When the request object refers to a role or cluster role, the verbs associated with the role's rules
ka.req.role.rules .resources	When the request object refers to a role or cluster role, the resources associated with the role's rules

Field name	Description
ka.req.service.type	When the request object refers to a service, the service type
ka.resp.name	The response object's name
ka.response.code	The response code
ka.response.reason	The response reason (usually present only for failures)

Conclusion

Congratulations, you are now a filtering expert! At this point, you should be able to read and understand Falco rules, and you are much closer to being able to write your own. In the next chapter, we will devote our attention to Falco's outputs.

CHAPTER 7

Falco Rules

Chapters 3 through 6 gave you a comprehensive view of Falco's architecture, describing most of the important concepts that a serious Falco user needs to understand. The remaining piece to cover is one of the most important ones: rules. Rules are at the heart of Falco. You've already encountered them several times, but this chapter approaches the topic in a more formal and comprehensive manner, giving you the foundation you will need as you work through the next parts of the book.

> This chapter covers what rules are and their syntax. The goal is to give you all the knowledge you need to understand and use them, not to teach you to write your own. Writing your own rules will be covered in Part IV of the book (in particular, in Chapter 13).

Falco is designed to be easy and intuitive, and the rule syntax and semantics are no exception. Rules files are straightforward, and you'll be able to understand them in no time. Let's start by covering some basics.

Introducing Falco Rules Files

Falco rules tell Falco what to do. They are typically packaged inside rules files, which Falco reads at startup time. A rules file is a YAML file that can contain one or more rules, with each rule being a node in the YAML body.

Falco comes packaged with a set of default rules files that are normally located in *etc/ falco*. The default rules files are loaded automatically if Falco is launched with no command-line options. These files are curated by the community and updated with every new release of Falco.

When it starts, Falco will tell you which rules files have been loaded:

```
$ sudo falco
Mon Jun  6 17:09:22 2022: Falco version 0.32.0 (driver version
39ae7d40496793cf3d3e7890c9bbdc202263836b)
Mon Jun  6 17:09:22 2022: Falco initialized with configuration file
/etc/falco/falco.yaml
Mon Jun  6 17:09:22 2022: Loading rules from file /etc/falco/falco_rules.yaml:
Mon Jun  6 17:09:22 2022: Loading rules from file
/etc/falco/falco_rules.local.yaml:
```

Often, you will want to load your own rules files instead of the default ones. You can do this in two different ways. The first one involves using the -r command-line option:

```
$ sudo falco -r book_rules_1.yaml -r book_rules_2.yaml
Mon Jun  6 17:10:17 2022: Falco version 0.32.0 (driver version
39ae7d40496793cf3d3e7890c9bbdc202263836b)
Mon Jun  6 17:10:17 2022: Falco initialized with configuration file
/etc/falco/falco.yaml
Mon Jun  6 17:10:17 2022: Loading rules from file book_rules_1.yaml:
Mon Jun  6 17:10:17 2022: Loading rules from file book_rules_2.yaml:
```

And the second one involves modifying the rules_file section of the Falco configuration file (normally located at */etc/falco/falco.yaml*), which looks like this by default:

```
rules_file:
  - /etc/falco/falco_rules.yaml
  - /etc/falco/falco_rules.local.yaml
  - /etc/falco/rules.d
```

You can add, remove, or modify entries in this section to control which rules files Falco loads.

Note that with both of these methods, you can specify a directory instead of a single file. For example:

```
$ sudo falco -r ~/my_rules_directory
```

and:

```
rules_file:
  - /home/john/my_rules_directory
```

This is handy because it lets you add and remove rules files by just altering the contents of a directory, without having to reconfigure Falco.

As we mentioned, Falco's default rules files are normally installed under */etc/falco*. This directory contains files that are critical for Falco to function in different environments. Table 7-1 gives an overview of the most important ones.

Table 7-1. Falco's default rules files

Filename	Description
falco_rules.yaml	This is Falco's main rules file, containing the official set of system call–based rules for hosts and containers.
falco_rules.local.yaml	This is where you can add your own rules, or create overrides to modify existing rules, without risking polluting *falco_rules.yaml*. Chapter 13 will cover rule creation and overriding in detail.
rules.available/ application_rules.yaml	This file contains rules that target common applications like Cassandra and Mongo. Since this ruleset tends to be fairly noisy, it's disabled by default.
k8s_audit_rules.yaml	This file contains rules that detect threats and misconfigurations by tapping into the Kubernetes audit log. This ruleset is not enabled by default; to use it, you need to enable it and configure the Falco Kubernetes Audit Events plugin (*https://oreil.ly/6aQEx*).
aws_cloudtrail_rules.yaml	This file contains rules that perform detections by tapping into the stream of AWS CloudTrail logs. This ruleset is not enabled by default; to use it, you need to enable it and configure the Falco CloudTrail plugin (*https://oreil.ly/1opUj*), as we will explain in Chapter 11.
rules.d	This empty directory is included in the default Falco configuration. This means you can add files to this directory (or create symlinks to your rules files in this directory) and Falco will automatically load them.

By default, Falco loads two of these files: *falco_rules.yaml* and *falco_rules.local.yaml*. In addition, it mounts the *rules.d* directory, which you can use to extend the ruleset with no changes to the command line or to the configuration file.

Anatomy of a Falco Rules File

Now that you know what a rules file looks like from the outside, it's time to learn what's inside it. The YAML in a rules file can contain three different types of nodes: *rules*, *macros*, and *lists*. Let's take a look at what these constructs are and the roles they play in rules files.

Rules

A rule declares a Falco detection. You've seen several examples in the previous chapters, but as a reminder, a rule has two main purposes:

1. Declare a condition that, when met, will cause the user to be notified

2. Define the output message that will be reported to the user when the condition is met

Here's an example rule, borrowed from Chapter 6:

```
- rule: File Becoming Executable by Others
  desc: Attempt to make a file executable by other users
  condition: >
    (evt.type=chmod or evt.type=fchmod or evt.type=fchmodat)
```

```
  and evt.arg.mode contains S_IXOTH
output: >
  attempt to make a file executable by others
  (file=%evt.arg.filename mode=%evt.arg.mode user=%user.name
  failed=%evt.failed)
priority: WARNING
source: syscall
tags: [filesystem, book]
```

This rule notifies us every time there is an attempt to change the permissions of a file to make it executable by another user.

As you can see in the preceding example, a rule contains several keys. Some of the keys are required, while others are optional. Table 7-2 contains a comprehensive list of the fields that you can use in a rule.

Table 7-2. Rule fields

Key	Required	Description
rule	Yes	A short sentence describing the rule and uniquely identifying it.
desc	Yes	A longer description that describes in more detail what the rule detects.
condition	Yes	The rule condition. This is a filter expression, with the syntax described in Chapter 6, specifying the condition that needs to be met in order for the rule to trigger.
output	Yes	A printf-like message that is emitted by Falco when the rule triggers.
priority	Yes	The priority of the alert generated when the rule is triggered. Falco uses syslog-style priorities and therefore accepts the following values for this key: EMERGENCY, ALERT, CRITICAL, ERROR, WARNING, NOTICE, INFORMATIONAL, and DEBUG.
source	No	The data source to which the rule should be applied. If this key is not present, the source is assumed to be syscall. Each plugin defines its own source type that can be used as the value for this key. For example, use aws_cloudtrail for rules that contain conditions/outputs based on the CloudTrail plugin fields.
enabled	No	A Boolean key that can optionally be used to disable a rule. Disabled rules are not loaded by the engine and don't require any resources when Falco is running. If this key is missing, enabled is assumed to be true.
tags	No	A list of tags that are associated with this rule. Tags have multiple uses, including easily selecting which rules to load and categorizing the alerts that Falco generates. We'll talk about tags later in this chapter.
warn_evttypes	No	When set to false, this flag disables warnings about missing event type checks for this rule. When Falco loads a rule, in addition to validating its syntax, it runs a number of checks to make sure that the rule meets basic performance criteria. If you know what you are doing and you specifically want to craft a rule that doesn't meet such criteria, this flag will prevent Falco from complaining. By default, the value of this flag is true.
skip-if-unknown-filter	No	Setting this flag to true causes Falco to silently skip this rule if the field is not accepted by the current version of the rule engine. If this flag is not set or set to false, Falco will print an error and exit when it encounters a rule that cannot be parsed.

The key fields in the rule are `condition` and `output`. Chapter 6 talks about them extensively, so if you haven't done so yet, we recommend that you consult that chapter for an overview.

Macros

Macros are heavily used in the default Falco ruleset. They make it possible to "separate" portions of rules into independent and reusable entities. You can think of a macro as a piece of a condition that has been separated out and can be referenced by name. To explore this concept, let's go back to the previous example and try to modularize it using a macro:

```
- rule: File Becoming Executable by Others
  desc: Attempt to make a file executable by other users
  condition: >
    (evt.type=chmod or evt.type=fchmod or evt.type=fchmodat)
    and evt.arg.mode contains S_IXOTH
  output: >
    attempt to make a file executable by others
    (file=%evt.arg.filename mode=%evt.arg.mode user=%user.name
    failed=%evt.failed)
  priority: WARNING
```

Take a look at the condition: we match the event type against three different system calls because, well, the kernel offers three different system calls to change file permissions. In practice, these three system calls are all flavors of chmod (*https://oreil.ly/qAdBA*), with essentially the same arguments to check. We can make the same condition easier to read by isolating this complexity into a macro:

```
- macro: chmod
  condition: (evt.type=chmod or evt.type=fchmod or evt.type=fchmodat)

- rule: File Becoming Executable by Others
  desc: attempt to make a file executable by other users
  condition: chmod and evt.arg.mode contains S_IXOTH
  output: >
    attempt to make a file executable by others
    (file=%evt.arg.filename mode=%evt.arg.mode user=%user.name
    failed=%evt.failed)
  priority: WARNING
```

Note how the condition is much shorter and more readable. In addition, now we can reuse the chmod macro in other rules, simplifying all of them and making them consistent. Even more importantly, if we ever want to add another chmod system call that Falco should inspect, we have only one place to change (the macro) instead of multiple rules.

Macros help us keep our rulesets clean, modular, and maintainable.

Lists

Like macros, lists are heavily used in Falco's default ruleset. Lists are collections of items that can be included from other parts of the ruleset. For example, lists can be included by rules, by macros, and even by other lists. The difference between a macro and a list is that the former is actually a condition and is parsed as a filtering expression. Lists, on the other hand, are more akin to arrays in a programming language.

Continuing with the previous example, an even better way to write it is the following:

```
- list: chmod_syscalls
  items: [chmod, fchmod, fchmodat]

- macro: chmod
  condition: (evt.type in (chmod_syscalls))

- rule: File Becoming Executable by Others
  desc: attempt to make a file executable by other users
  condition: chmod and evt.arg.mode contains S_IXOTH
  output: >
    attempt to make a file executable by others
    (file=%evt.arg.filename mode=%evt.arg.mode user=%user.name
    failed=%evt.failed)
```

What's different this time? First, we've changed the chmod macro to use the in operator instead of doing three separate comparisons. This not only is more efficient, but it also gives us the opportunity to separate out the three system calls into a list. The list approach is great for rule maintenance because it allows us to isolate only the values into an array-like representation that is clear and compact and can easily be overridden if necessary (more on list overriding in Chapter 13).

Rule Tagging

Tagging is the concept of assigning labels to rules. If you are familiar with modern cloud computing environments like AWS or Kubernetes, you know that they let you attach labels to resources. Doing that lets you manage those resources more easily, as groups instead of individuals. Tagging brings the same philosophy to Falco rules: it lets you treat rules as cattle instead of pets.

This, for example, is a rule in the default Falco ruleset:

```
- rule: Launch Privileged Container
  desc: >
    Detect the initial process started in a privileged container.
    Exceptions are made for known trusted images.
  condition: >
    container_started and container
    and container.privileged=true
    and not falco_privileged_containers
```

```
      and not user_privileged_containers
   output: >
      Privileged container started
      (user=%user.name user_loginuid=%user.loginuid command=%proc.cmdline
      %container.info image=%container.image.repository:%container.image.tag)
   priority: INFO
   tags: [container, cis, mitre_privilege_escalation, mitre_lateral_movement]
```

Note how the rule has several tags, some indicating what the rule applies to (e.g., `container`) and others mapping it to compliance frameworks like CIS and MITRE ATT&CK.

Falco lets you use tags to control which rules are loaded. This is done through two command-line flags, `-T` and `-t`. Here's how it works:

- Use `-T` to disable rules with a specific tag. For example, to skip all rules with the `k8s` and `cis` tags, you can run Falco like this:

  $ sudo falco -T k8s -T cis

- Use `-t` for the opposite purpose; i.e., to only run the rules that have the specified tag. For example, to only run the rules with the `k8s` and `cis` tags, you can use the following command line:

  $ sudo falco -t k8s -T cis

Both `-T` and `-t` can be specified multiple times on the command line.

You can use any tags you want to decorate your rules. However, the default ruleset is standardized on a coherent set of tags. Table 7-3 shows what this standard set of tags is, according to the official Falco documentation.

Table 7-3. Default rule tags

Tag	Used for
file	Rules related to reading/writing files and accessing filesystems
software_mgmt	Rules related to package management (rpm, dpkg, etc.) or to installing new software
process	Rules related to processes, command execution, and interprocess communication (IPC)
database	Rules that have to do with databases
host	Rules that apply to virtual and physical machines but *not* to containers
shell	Rules that apply to starting shells and performing shell operations
container	Rules that apply to containers and don't work for hosts
k8s	Rules related to Kubernetes
users	Rules that apply to users, groups, and identity management
network	Rules detecting network activity
cis	Rules covering portions of the CIS benchmark

Tag	Used for
`mitre_*`	Rules covering the MITRE ATT&CK framework (this is a category that includes several tags: `mitre_execution`, `mitre_persistence`, `mitre_privilege_escalation`, and so on)

Declaring the Expected Engine Version

If you open a Falco rules file with a text editor, the first line you will normally see is a statement that looks like this:

```
- required_engine_version: 9
```

Declaring the minimum required engine version is optional, but it's very important because it helps ensure that the version of Falco you are running will properly support the rules inside it. Some of the fields used in a ruleset may not exist in older versions of Falco, or a rule may require a system call that was added only recently. Without correct versioning, a rules file might not load or, even worse, it might load but produce incorrect results. If the rules file requires an engine version higher than the one supported by Falco, Falco will report an error and refuse to start.

Similarly, rules files can declare the plugin versions they are compatible with through the `required_plugin_versions` top-level field. This field is optional too; if you don't include it, no plugin compatibility checks will be performed, and you may see similar behavior to that just described. The syntax of `required_plugin_versions` is as follows:

```
- required_plugin_versions:
  - name: <plugin_name>
    version: <x.y.z>
  ...
```

Below `required_plugin_versions` you specify a list of objects, each of which has two properties: `name` and `version`. If a plugin is loaded and a corresponding entry in `required_plugin_versions` is found, then the loaded plugin version must be semver-compatible (*https://semver.org*) with the `version` property.

The default rules files that come prepackaged with Falco are all versioned. Don't forget to do the same in each of your rules files!

Replacing, Appending to, and Disabling Rules

Falco comes prepackaged with a rich and constantly growing set of rules that covers many important use cases. However, there are many situations where you might find it beneficial to customize the default ruleset. For example, you might want to decrease the noisiness of some rules, or you might be interested in expanding the scope of some of the Falco detections to better match your environment.

One way to approach these situations is to edit the default rules files. An important lesson to learn is that you don't have to do this. Actually, you *shouldn't* do this— Falco offers a more versatile way to customize rules, designed to make your changes maintainable and reusable across releases. Let's take a look at how this works.

Replacing Macros, Lists, and Rules

Replacing a list, macro, or rule is just a matter of redeclaring it. The second declaration can be in the same file, or in a separate file that is loaded after the one containing the original declaration.

Let's see how this works through an example. The following rule detects if a text editor has been opened as root (which, as we all know, people should avoid doing):

```
- list: editors
  items: [vi, nano]

- macro: editor_started
  condition: (evt.type = execve and proc.name in (editors))

- rule: Text Editor Run by Root
  desc: the root user opened a text editor
  condition: editor_started and user.name=root
  output: the root user started a text editor (cmdline=%proc.cmdline)
  priority: WARNING
```

If we save this rule in a rules file called *rulefile.yaml*, we can test the rule by loading the file in Falco:

```
$ sudo falco -r rulefile.yaml
```

The rule will trigger every time we run vi or nano as root.

Now say we want to change the rule to support a different set of text editors. We can create a second rules file, name it *editors.yaml*, and populate it in the following way:

```
- list: editors
  items: [emacs, subl]
```

Note how we redefined the content of the `editors` list, replacing the original command names with `emacs` and `subl`. Now we just load *editors.yaml* after the original rules file:

```
$ sudo falco -r rulefile.yaml -r editors.yaml
```

Falco will pick up the second definition of `editors` and generate an alert when root runs either emacs or subl, but *not* vi or nano. Essentially, we've replaced the content of the list.

This trick works exactly the same way with macros and rules as well.

Appending to Macros, Lists, and Rules

Let's stick to the same text editor rule example. This time, however, suppose we want to *append* additional names to the list of editors instead of replacing the full list. The mechanism is the same, but with the addition of the append keyword. Here is the syntax:

```
- list: editors
  items: [emacs, subl]
  append: true
```

We can save this list in a file named *additional_editors.yaml*. Now, if we run the following command line:

```
$ sudo falco -r rulefile.yaml -r editors.yaml
```

Falco will detect root execution of vi, nano, emacs, and subl.

You can append (using the same syntax) to macros and rules as well. However, there are a couple of things to keep in mind:

- For rules, it is only possible to append to the condition. Attempts to append to other keys, like output, will be ignored.

- Remember that appending to a condition just attaches the new text at the end of it, so be careful about ambiguities.

For example, suppose we extended the rule condition in our example by appending to it like this:

```
- rule: Text Editor Run by Root
  condition: or user.name = loris
  append: true
```

The full rule condition would become:

```
condition: editor_started and user.name=root or user.name = loris
```

This condition is clearly ambiguous. Will the rule trigger only whenever the user root or loris opens a text editor? Or will it trigger when root opens a text editor and when loris executes *any* command? To avoid such ambiguities, and to make your rules files more readable, you can use parentheses in the original conditions.

Disabling Rules

You will often encounter situations where you need to disable one or more rules in a ruleset, for example because they are too noisy or they are just not relevant for your environment. Falco provides different ways to do this. We are going to cover two of them: using the command line and overriding the enabled flag.

Disabling rules from the command line

Falco actually offers two separate ways to disable rules via the command line. The first one, which we discussed when talking about rule tagging earlier in this chapter, involves using the -T flag. As a refresher, you can use -T to disable rules with the given tag. -T can be used multiple times on the command line to disable multiple tags. For example, to skip all rules with either the k8s tag, the cis tag, or both, you can run Falco like this:

```
$ sudo falco -T k8s -T cis
```

The second way to disable rules from the command line is by using the -D flag. -D *<substring>* disables all the rules that include *<substring>* in their name. Similarly to -T, -D can be specified multiple times with different arguments.

These parameters can also be specified as a Helm chart value (extraArgs) if you are deploying Falco via the official Helm chart.

Disabling rules by overriding the enabled flag

You might remember from Table 7-2 that one of the optional rule fields is called enabled. As a refresher, here's how we documented it earlier in the chapter:

> A Boolean key that can optionally be used to disable a rule. Disabled rules are not loaded by the engine and don't require any resources when Falco is running. If this key is missing, enabled is assumed to be true.

enabled can be turned on or off by overriding the rule with the usual mechanism. For example, if you want to disable the *User mgmt binaries* rule in */etc/falco/falco_rules.yaml*, you can add the following content in */etc/falco/falco_rules.local.yaml*:

```
- rule: User mgmt binaries
  enabled: false
```

Conclusion

You see, it wasn't that hard! At this point, you should be able to read and understand Falco rules, and you are much closer to being able to write your own. We'll focus on rule writing in Part IV of the book, and in particular in Chapter 13. Our next step will be learning everything about Falco outputs.

CHAPTER 8

The Output Framework

In previous chapters, you learned how Falco collects events (its input) and how it processes them to allow you to receive important security notifications (its output). At the end of this processing pipeline, a key piece of Falco—the *output framework*—enables it to deliver those notifications (also called *alerts*) to the right place. We call it a framework because its modular design provides all you need to deliver notifications to any destination you wish. In this chapter, you will learn how the output framework works and how you can configure and extend it.

Falco's Output Architecture

The output framework is the last piece of the event-processing pipeline that we have been describing in this part of the book. Falco's user-space program implements the core mechanism internally, but external tools can extend it. Its job is to deliver notifications to the correct destination on time. Whenever an upstream event (produced by a driver, a plugin, or any other input source supported by Falco) meets a rule's condition, the rule engine asks the output framework to send a notification to a downstream consumer, which could be any other program or system in your environment (or simply you).

The process of delivering alerts involves two distinct stages, as pictured in Figure 8-1.

In the first stage, a *handler* receives the event data and information about the event-triggered rule. It prepares the notification using the provided information and formats the textual representation according to the rule's output key. Then, to prevent the output destination from blocking the processing pipeline (which runs in the main execution thread), the handler pushes the notification into a concurrent queue.[1] The push operation is nonblocking, so the processing pipeline does not need to wait for the notification consumer to pull the notification; it can continue to do its job without interruption. Indeed, Falco needs to perform this stage as quickly as possible so that the processing pipeline can process the next event.

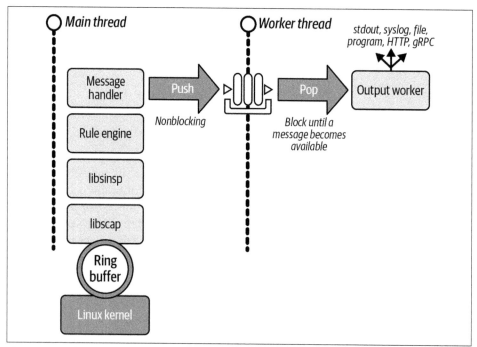

Figure 8-1. The two stages of delivering notifications in Falco

At the other end of the queue, the *output worker* (which runs in a separate execution thread) is waiting to pop notifications from the queue. This is when the second stage begins. Once the output worker receives a notification, it immediately fans that notification out to all configured output channels. An *output channel* (or simply an *output*) is a part of the output framework that allows Falco to forward alerts to a destination. Each output channel implements the actual logic to notify a particular class of alert consumers. For instance, some consumers want notifications written to a file, while others prefer them to be posted to a web endpoint (see Chapter 10).

---

1 A *concurrent queue* is a way of implementing a queue data structure (*https://oreil.ly/NWtzd*) that multiple running threads can safely access in parallel. The *pop* and *push* operations are typical actions that a queue supports (respectively, to enqueue and dequeue an item). Most implementations allow performing those operations in either blocking or nonblocking fashions.

This two-stage approach allows the processing pipeline to run without interference from the output delivery process. However, things can still go wrong with delivery. In particular, when delivering a notification involves I/O operations, those may block the caller temporarily (for example, in the event of a network slowdown) or indefinitely (e.g., when there's no space left on the disk). The queue in the middle of the two stages works well at absorbing temporary slowdowns—so well that you won't even notice them (by default, Falco can accumulate pending notifications in the queue for up to two seconds). But when the recipient of a notification blocks for a long time (or indefinitely), there's nothing that Falco can automatically do. As a last resort, it will try to inform you about what happened by logging to the standard error stream (*stderr*) (*https://oreil.ly/IbBik*). When this happens, it is usually a symptom of a misconfiguration (for example, the path to the destination is wrong) or insufficient resources (no space left in the destination), which the user is asked to manually fix.

Once the notification delivery process completes, Falco's user-space program has accomplished its purpose. It's then up to the consumer to decide what to do with the alert.

The output framework accommodates many different use cases and can take care of many possible issues. It is also flexible enough to allow you to receive notifications in various ways and at different destinations. The rest of this chapter will give you details about all the available possibilities. We'll also take a quick look at some other tools that allow you to further extend output processing before delivering the notifications to their final destination. (We'll go deeper into this in Chapter 13.)

Output Formatting

In the first stage of notification delivery, Falco applies formatting to the notification before forwarding it to the output channel. You can customize how Falco presents notifications to its consumers so that you can easily integrate them with your specific use case.

Two options in the Falco configuration file (*/etc/falco/falco.yaml*) control this operation. The first controls the formatting of the timestamp:

```
time_format_iso_8601: false
```

If this option is `false` (the default value), Falco will display dates and times according to the */etc/localtime* settings. If it's `true` (the default value when Falco is running in a container), Falco will use the ISO 8601 standard for representing dates and times. Note that this option controls not only output notifications but also any other messages that Falco logs.

The second option is actually a set of options that enable JSON formatting for the notifications. By default, JSON formatting is disabled:

```
json_output: false
```

With this setting, Falco formats the notification as a plain-text string (including the timestamp, the severity, and the message). If it's set to `true`, Falco encloses the notification in a JSON-formatted string, including several fields. The following two options allow you to include or exclude some of those fields from the output:

```
json_include_output_property: true
```
> If this option is enabled (the default), you will still find the plain-text representation of the notification in the `output` field of the JSON object. You can disable this option to save a few bytes if you don't need it.

```
json_include_tags_property: true
```
> If this option is enabled, you will find a `tags` field in the JSON object containing an array of tags specified in the matching rule. Rules with no tags defined will have an empty array (`tags:[]`) in the output. If you disable this option, you won't get the `tags` field in the JSON object.

> Despite its name, `json_output` is not an output channel. The `json_output` configuration controls the formatting applied to notifications in the first stage of processing—thus, it affects the content of the notifications that channels deliver. The next section describes the available output channels.

Output Channels

Falco comes with six built-in output channels, listed in Table 8-1. We will describe each of them in more detail in the following subsections. By default only two channels are enabled—standard output (*https://oreil.ly/kBm4I*) and syslog output—but Falco allows you to enable as many channels as you need simultaneously.

Table 8-1. Falco's built-in output channels

Channel	Description
Standard output	Sends notifications to Falco's standard output (stdout)
Syslog output	Sends notifications to the system via syslog
File output	Writes notifications to a file
Program output	Pipes notifications to a program's standard input
HTTP output	Posts notifications to a URL
gRPC output	Allows a client program to consume notifications via a gRPC API

You configure these outputs in the Falco configuration file (*/etc/falco/falco.yaml*). Note that all the configuration snippets in this section are part of this file.

Each output channel has at least one option called `enabled`, which can be `true` or `false`. Other options may be available for specific outputs (you will discover them soon). Furthermore, there are some global options that can affect the functioning of all or some output channels. One such option (which you saw in the previous section) is `json_output`; when this is enabled, the alert messages will be JSON-formatted, regardless of the output channel used. The other global options that can affect the output channels' behavior are listed in Table 8-2.

Table 8-2. Global options for output channels

Global option (with default)	Description
`buffered_outputs:` `false`	This option enables or disables full buffering in output channels. When disabled, Falco immediately flushes the output buffer on every alert, which may generate higher CPU usage but is useful when piping outputs into another process or a script. Unless you encounter an issue with the default value, you usually won't need to enable this option. Note that Falco's `--unbuffered` command-line flag can override this option. Not all output channels observe this global option. Some output channels may implement specific buffering strategies that you cannot disable.
`output_timeout: 2000`	The value of this option specifies the duration to wait (in milliseconds) before considering the delivery notification deadline exceeded. When the notification consumer blocks and the output channel cannot deliver an alert within the given deadline, Falco reports an error indicating which output is blocking the notifications. Such an error indicates a misconfiguration issue or I/O problem in the consumer that Falco cannot recover.

`outputs:`
`  rate: 1`
`  max_burst: 1000`
	These options control the notification rate limiter so that output channels do not flood their destinations. The rate limiter implements a token bucket algorithm. To send a notification, the system must remove a token from the bucket. `rate` sets the number of tokens the system gains per second, and `max_burst` sets the maximum number of tokens in the bucket.
	With the defaults, Falco can send up to 1,000 notifications in a row; then it must wait for additional tokens to be added to the bucket, which happens at the rate of 1 token per second. In other words, once the bucket has been emptied, notifications are rate-limited to one per second.

 Although not strictly related to the output mechanism, other Falco settings may affect what you will receive in the output. For example, the configuration `priority: <severity>` controls the minimum rule priority level to load and run, and the command-line option `-t <tag>` allows you to load only those rules with a specific tag. In those cases, clearly, you won't get any output regarding rules that Falco does not load. In general, any rules-related option or configuration could indirectly affect the output.

Now that you've learned what the output channels are and what settings can change their behavior, let's go through each in turn.

Standard Output

Standard output (`stdout_output` in the configuration file, enabled by default) is Falco's most straightforward output channel. When it is enabled, Falco will print a line to standard output for each alert. This allows you to see alert notifications when manually running Falco from a console or when looking at a container or Kubernetes Pod log. The only option specifically available for this output channel is `enabled` (which can be either `true` or `false`). However, it's also affected by the global buffering option, `buffered_outputs`. When the outputs are buffered, the stdout stream will be fully buffered or line-buffered if the stream is an interactive device (such as a TTY).

Syslog Output

The syslog output channel (`syslog_output` in the configuration file, also enabled by default) allows Falco to send a syslog message for each alert. As with standard output, the only option specifically available for this output channel is `enabled` (which can be either `true` or `false`). When enabled, Falco sends messages to syslog with a facility of `LOG_USER`[2] and a severity level equal to the priority value defined by the rule.

Depending on the syslog daemon you are using, you can read those messages using commands like `tail -f /var/log/syslog` or `journalctl -xe`. The actual message format depends on the syslog daemon, too.

File Output

If you enable file output, Falco will write each alert to a file. The default configuration for this output channel is:

```
file_output:
  enabled: false
  keep_alive: false
  filename: ./events.txt
```

The `filename` option allows you to specify the destination file to which Falco will write. It will create the file if it does not yet exist and will not try to truncate or rotate the file if it exists already.

With `keep_alive` disabled (the default), Falco will open the file for appending, write the message, and then close the file for each alert. If `keep_alive` is set to `true`, Falco will only open the file once before the first alert and will keep it open for all subsequent alerts. Whether `keep_alive` is enabled or not, Falco closes and reopens

---

2 In the syslog protocol, the facility value determines the function of the process that created the message. `LOG_USER` is intended for messages generated by user-level applications.

the file when it receives a SIGUSR1 signal. This feature is handy if you'd like to use a program to rotate the output file (for example, logrotate).

Finally, writing to a file is generally buffered unless you disable the global buffering option. Closing the file will flush the buffer.

Program Output

The program output is very similar to the file output, but in this case Falco will write the content of each alert to the standard input of a program you specify in the configuration file. The default configuration for this output channel is:

```
program_output:
  enabled: false
  keep_alive: false
  program: >
    jq '{text: .output}' | curl -d @- -X POST https://hooks.slack.com/services...
```

The program field allows you to specify the program the alerts will be sent to. Falco runs the program via a shell, so you can specify a command pipeline if you wish to add any processing steps before delivering the messages to the program. This field's default value shows a nice example of its usage: when executed, that one-liner posts the alert to a Slack webhook endpoint. (However, using Falcosidekick would be a better option; see Chapter 12.)

If keep_alive is set to false, Falco restarts the program and writes the content of the alert to its standard input each time it has a notification to deliver. If keep_alive is set to true, Falco starts the program once (right before sending the first alert) and keeps the program pipe open for delivering subsequent alerts.

Falco closes and reopens the program when it receives a SIGUSR1 signal. However, the program runs in the same process group as Falco, so it gets all of the signals that Falco receives. It's up to you to override the program signal handler if you need to.

Buffering is supported via the global option. When Falco closes the program, it also flushes the buffer.

HTTP Output

When you need to send alerts over an HTTP(S) connection, the best choice is to use the HTTP output. Its default configuration is straightforward:

```
http_output:
  enabled: false
  url: http://some.url
```

Once enabled, the only other configuration you need to specify is the url of your endpoint. Falco will make an HTTP POST request to the specified URL for each alert.

Both unencrypted HTTP and secure HTTPS endpoints are supported. Buffering for this output channel is always enabled (even if you disable the global buffering option).

The HTTP output channel is preferred when you use Falcosidekick; it takes Falco's alerts and forwards them in fan-out style to many different destinations (more than 50 are available at the time of writing). If you want Falco to forward alerts to Falcosidekick, apply this Falco configuration:

```
json_output: true
json_include_output_property: true
http_output:
  enabled: true
  url: "http://localhost:2801/"
```

Note that this configuration assumes you already have Falcosidekick running and configured to listen to localhost:2801; change it accordingly if your setup is different. You can find details about configuring Falcosidekick in Chapter 12 and in its online documentation (*https://oreil.ly/uUQBR*).

gRPC Output

The gRPC (*https://grpc.io*) output is the most sophisticated output channel. It allows greater control than the others over alert forwarding and full granularity in the information received. This output channel is for you if you'd like to send alerts to an external program connected via Falco's gRCP API. Its default configuration is:

```
grpc_output:
  enabled: false
```

As you can see, it's disabled by default—and before you enable it, there's something you should consider. Falco comes with a gRPC server that exposes the API. You will need to enable both the gRPC server and the gRPC output (we will show you how to do that in a moment). The API provides several gRPC services, only some of which are related to the gRPC output. One service allows you to pull all pending alerts. Another allows you to subscribe to a stream of alerts. Client programs can decide which implementations best fit their needs. In both cases, when the gRPC output is enabled, Falco uses an internal queue to temporarily store alerts until the client program consumes them. This means you should not enable the gRPC output if there's no client program set up to consume the alerts; otherwise, the internal queue may grow indefinitely. The global buffering option does not affect this output channel.

With that in mind, to make this output channel work, the first thing you have to do is to enable the gRPC server. It supports two binding types: over a Unix socket and over the network with mandatory mutual TLS authentication.

Here's how to enable the gRPC server over a Unix socket:

```
grpc:
  enabled: true
  bind_address: "unix:///var/run/falco.sock"
  threadiness: 0
```

And here's how to enable the gRPC server over the network with mandatory mutual TLS authentication:

```
grpc:
  enabled: true
  bind_address: "0.0.0.0:5060"
  threadiness: 0
  private_key: "/etc/falco/certs/server.key"
  cert_chain: "/etc/falco/certs/server.crt"
  root_certs: "/etc/falco/certs/ca.crt"
```

Both binding types offer the same gRPC functionalities, so you can choose the one that satisfies your needs. Once you have enabled the gRPC server, the next step is to enable the gRCP output:

```
grpc_output:
  enabled: true
```

Finally, you will have to configure your client program to connect to the Falco gRPC API. How this is done depends on the program you are using. The Falcosecurity organization provides two programs that can connect to this output (see Chapter 2): falco-exporter (*https://oreil.ly/FN9gE*), which connects to the Falco gRPC API to export metrics consumable by Prometheus (more on this in Chapter 12), and the event-generator (*https://oreil.ly/4MHw1*), which can optionally connect to the Falco gRPC API to test whether fake events are actually processed (helpful when developing integration tests). You can also implement your own program. The Falcosecurity organization provides SDKs that allow you to create gRPC client programs for Falco easily in several programming languages—for example, client-go for Golang (*https://oreil.ly/HXPKL*), client-rs for Rust (*https://oreil.ly/XdgVp*), and client-py for Python (*https://oreil.ly/A64Dh*). You can find more information about developing with the Falco gRPC API in Chapter 14.

Last but not least, here is an extract from the proto-definition of the message that Falco sends via the gRCP API:

```
// The `response` message is the representation of the output model.
// It contains all the elements that Falco emits in an output along
// with the definitions for priorities and source.
message response {
  google.protobuf.Timestamp time = 1;
  falco.schema.priority priority = 2;
  falco.schema.source source_deprecated = 3 [deprecated=true];
  string rule = 4;
  string output = 5;
  map<string, string> output_fields = 6;
  string hostname = 7;
```

```
    repeated string tags = 8;
    string source = 9;
}
```

The `response` message includes the already formatted alert string (which you will find in the `output` field) as well as all the component pieces of information, split across various fields. The client program can assemble and process them in any way it needs, which is very useful if you want to build your own application on top of Falco.

Other Logging Options

So far we've described the core part of the output framework. Now let's look at a few options to help you in troubleshooting. Like most applications, Falco can output debugging information and errors. Those informative messages are about the functioning of Falco itself and are not its primary output.

Falco implements various logging messages internally. They can vary from one release to another. A common example of this logging is the initial information that Falco prints out when it starts. Another, less common case is when Falco informs you that it was not able to load the driver:

```
Mon Dec 20 14:00:23 2021: Unable to load the driver.
```

The term *logging* does *not* refer to the process of outputting security notifications. The log messages discussed in this section are not security alerts. Logging options do not affect notification processing in any way. Also, since these log messages are not notifications, Falco does not output them through the output channels. Although you might see the usual notifications interleaved with log messages when running Falco in a terminal, keep in mind that they are different.

Falco outputs these messages via the standard error stream (*https://oreil.ly/yatpB*) and sends them to syslog. You can configure Falco to discard some messages based on their severity level. Table 8-3 lists the logging options you can configure in Falco's configuration file (*/etc/falco/falco.yaml*).

Table 8-3. Options for Falco's internal logging

Logging option (with default)	Description
`log_stderr: true`	If enabled, Falco sends log messages to the stderr.
`log_syslog: true`	If enabled, Falco sends log messages to syslog. Note that this option is not related to the syslog output and does not affect it.

Logging option (with default)	Description
`log_level: info`	This option defines the minimum log level to include in logs: `emergency`, `alert`, `critical`, `error`, `warning`, `notice`, `info`, or `debug`. Note that these values, although similar, are not rule priority levels.

Conclusion

This chapter concludes Part II of this book. At this point, you should have a solid understanding of Falco's architecture and its inner workings. Your familiarity with the processing pipeline's data flow, ending with the output framework, will allow you to use Falco in a variety of ways. For example, you can view security notifications in your favorite dashboard or even create a response engine (a mechanism that takes action when a specific event occurs) on top of Falco. To discover more use cases, use your imagination—and continue reading this book.

The next level up is real-world use cases, so Part III is all about running Falco in production. As always, we will guide you through each step.

PART III

Running Falco in Production

CHAPTER 9

Installing Falco

Welcome to Part III of this book, which will walk you through using Falco in the real world. Now that you know how Falco and its architecture work, the next step is to start using it to protect your applications and systems. In this chapter, you will learn what you need to know to install Falco in production. We will show you different scenarios and common best practices so that you can find the right instructions for your use case.

We'll start by giving you an overview of common usage scenarios, then we'll describe different installation methods for each of them. We strongly recommend reading about all of the installation methods, even if you need only some of them, to get a complete picture of the possibilities and choose which fits your needs best.

Choosing Your Setup

The Falco Project officially supports three ways to run Falco in production:

- Running Falco directly on a host
- Running Falco in a container
- Deploying Falco to a Kubernetes cluster

Each option has a different installation method, and there are a few important differences between the first option and the others. Installing Falco directly on the host is your *only* choice when your environment does not include a container runtime or Kubernetes. It is also the most secure way to run Falco, because it's isolated from the container system (and thus difficult to breach in case of compromise). However, installing Falco directly on the host is usually the most difficult solution to maintain. It's also not always possible (for example, when your applications live in a managed Kubernetes cluster and you don't have full access to the host machines). The other options are usually more straightforward and easier to manage. Especially if your applications run on a Kubernetes cluster, deploying Falco to Kubernetes is a common choice. Consider the pros and cons of each and your requirements before making your choice.

Before installing Falco with any of these methods, you need to decide how you're going to use Falco, which can have a significant impact on the installation process and configuration. The two most common scenarios are monitoring syscalls and working with data sources provided by plugins.

The default scenario is instrumenting the system to monitor syscalls. In this case you will need to deploy a Falco sensor on each machine or cluster node, as well as installing a driver on each underlying host.

When you work with data sources provided by plugins, you will likely need to install only one Falco sensor (or one for each event producer), and you won't need a driver. Although there may be small differences in the actual setup of each data source, for simplicity we can treat this as a single installation scenario because the overall process is very similar. Generally, this latter scenario has fewer requirements and is simpler to implement.

If you need to satisfy more than one scenario at the same time, you will need more Falco installations. You can then aggregate the notifications coming from each sensor by using other tools, like Falcosidekick (discussed in Chapter 12).

Your final setup will depend on your needs and choices. The following sections provide instructions for each installation method in the two scenarios mentioned above (monitoring syscalls and working with data sources provided by plugins).

Installing Directly on the Host

Installing Falco directly on a host is a straightforward task—you learned the essential aspects in Chapter 2. This installation method is mainly intended for the default scenario where Falco uses system calls to secure and monitor a system, so it also installs the driver and configures Falco to use it. (In Chapter 10, we'll discuss how to change the Falco configuration and set it up for other data sources.)

This method installs the following:

- The user-space program *falco*
- The driver (the kernel module, by default)
- The default configuration file and the default ruleset files in */etc/falco*
- The *falco-driver-loader* utility (you can use this to manage the driver)
- A few bundled plugins (these may vary from version to version)

To install Falco, you will use one of the following artifacts provided by Falco's "Download" page (*https://oreil.ly/sOLzu*):

- *.rpm* package
- *.deb* package
- *.tar.gz* (binary) package

You should use one of the first two packages if you intend to install Falco via a compatible package manager; otherwise, use the binary package. Read on for more details.

> The following subsections include various commands that you need to run on your system. Ensure that you have sufficient privileges to execute them (for example, using sudo).

Using a Package Manager

This installation method is for Linux distributions with a package manager that supports *.deb* or *.rpm* packages. The setup process for a *.deb* or *.rpm* package will also install a systemd unit to use Falco as a service on your system, as well as the kernel module—the default driver—via Dynamic Kernel Module Support (dkms).

apt and *yum* are the most popular package managers that allow installing, respectively, *.deb* and *.rpm* packages. If you're using a different package manager that supports *.deb* or *.rpm* packages, the installation procedure will be very similar, though the exact instructions may vary. Refer to its documentation for further details.

Using apt (.deb package)

apt is the default package manager for Debian and Debian-based distributions like Ubuntu. It allows you to install software applications distributed as *.deb* packages. To install Falco using apt, you first need to trust The Falco Project's GPG key (*https://oreil.ly/Egkoo*) and configure the apt repository that holds Falco packages:

```
$ curl -s https://falco.org/repo/falcosecurity-3672BA8F.asc | apt-key add -
$ echo "deb https://download.falco.org/packages/deb stable main" | tee \
    -a /etc/apt/sources.list.d/falcosecurity.list
```

Then update the apt package list:

```
$ apt-get update -y
```

Since this installation method will also install Falco's kernel module, you must install the Linux kernel headers as a precondition:

```
$ apt-get -y install linux-headers-$(uname -r)
```

Finally, install Falco:

```
$ apt-get install -y falco
```

Using yum (.rpm package)

yum is a command-line utility for Linux distributions that use the RPM Package Manager, such as CentOS, RHEL, Fedora, and Amazon Linux. It allows you to install software applications distributed as *.rpm* packages. Before installing Falco with yum, you must ensure that the make package and the dkms package are present on your system. You can check that by running:

```
$ yum list make dkms
```

If they are not present, install them:

```
$ yum install epel-release
$ yum install make dkms
```

Next, trust The Falco Project's GPG key (*https://oreil.ly/t5WaG*) and configure the RPM repository that holds Falco packages:

```
$ rpm --import https://falco.org/repo/falcosecurity-3672BA8F.asc
$ curl -s -o /etc/yum.repos.d/falcosecurity.repo \
    https://falco.org/repo/falcosecurity-rpm.repo
```

Since this installation method will also install Falco's kernel module, you must install the Linux kernel headers as a precondition:

```
$ yum -y install kernel-devel-$(uname -r)
```

> If yum -y install kernel-devel-$(uname -r) does not find the kernel headers package, run yum distro-sync and then reboot the system. After the reboot, try the preceding command again.

Finally, install Falco:

```
$ yum -y install falco
```

Completing the installation

You should now have the kernel module installed via dkms and a systemd unit installed to run Falco as a service.

Before you start using Falco, you need to enable the Falco systemd service:

```
$ systemctl enable falco
```

Your installation is now complete. The service will automatically start running at the next reboot. If you want to start it immediately, just run:

```
$ systemctl start falco
```

From now on, you can manage the Falco service through the functions provided by systemd.

Switching to the eBPF probe

Falco packages use the kernel module by default, and this is usually the best choice when installing Falco directly on the host. However, if you have particular requirements or other reasons not to use the kernel module, you can easily switch to the eBPF probe.

First, make sure you have an eBPF probe installed on your system. You can install it using the *falco-driver-loader* script, as explained in "Managing the Driver" on page 122.

Then you need to edit the systemd unit file, located at */usr/lib/systemd/user/falco.service* (the path may vary depending on your distro). You can use `systemctl edit falco` to modify it. You need to add an option to set the `FALCO_BPF_PROBE` environment variable in the [`Service`] section of that file. Also, in the same section, comment (or remove) the `ExecStartPre` and `ExecStartPost` options, so the Falco service will not load the kernel module anymore. The changes are highlighted in the following excerpt from the *falco.service* file:

```
[Unit]
Description=Falco: Container Native Runtime Security
Documentation=https://falco.org/docs/

[Service]
Type=simple
User=root
Environment='FALCO_BPF_PROBE=""'
#ExecStartPre=/sbin/modprobe falco
ExecStart=/usr/bin/falco --pidfile=/var/run/falco.pid
#ExecStopPost=/sbin/rmmod falco
```

Once you're done, don't forget to restart the Falco service:

```
$ systemctl restart falco
```

Falco should now start using the eBPF probe.

Using a plugin

Falco packages come configured for the syscalls instrumentation scenario, so the included systemd unit loads the kernel module when Falco starts. However, if you're not using syscalls, you don't need to load the driver. As described in the previous section, to prevent the Falco service from loading the kernel module, edit the */usr/lib/systemd/user/falco.service* file and remove (or comment out) the `ExecStartPre` and

`ExecStartPost` options. Optionally, you can also configure the service to run Falco with a less privileged user by modifying the value of the `User` option.

Next, you'll need to configure Falco to use the plugin of your choice (we'll explain how to do this in Chapter 10) and restart the Falco service. Falco will then run using the new configuration.

Without Using a Package Manager

Installing Falco without using a package manager is quick and easy. This installation method is intended for distributions that do not support a compatible package manager. We walked through the steps in detail in Chapter 2, but we'll give you a short refresher here.

All you need to do is grab the link to the latest available version of the binary package from the Falco "Download" page (*https://oreil.ly/HEvdB*), and download it into a local folder:

```
$ curl -L -O \
    https://download.falco.org/packages/bin/x86_64/falco-0.32.0-x86_64.tar.gz
```

Then extract the package and copy its content to your filesystem's root:

```
$ tar -xvf falco-0.32.0-x86_64.tar.gz
$ cp -R falco-0.32.0-x86_64/* /
```

Finally, if you're planning to use system calls as your data source, install the driver manually before using Falco (you'll find instructions in the following section). You don't need to install the driver if you want to use a plugin. Also note that the binary package does not provide a systemd unit or any other mechanism to run Falco when your system starts automatically, so whether to execute Falco or run it as a service is entirely up to you.

Managing the Driver

If you use syscalls as a data source, you will likely need to manage the driver. If you installed Falco without a package manager, you'll have to install the driver before using Falco manually. All the available packages provide a helpful script called *falco-driver-loader* (introduced in Chapter 2) that you can use for this purpose. If you followed the instructions earlier in this chapter, you should already have it installed on your system.

Our suggestion is to familiarize yourself with the script by using `--help` to get its command-line usage. To do that, just run:

```
$ falco-driver-loader --help
```

The script allows you to perform several actions, including installing a driver (either the kernel module or the eBPF probe) by compiling it or downloading it. It also allows you to remove a previously installed driver.

If you run the script without any options:

```
$ falco-driver-loader
```

by default it will try to install a kernel module via dkms. To be precise, it will first try to download a prebuilt driver, if one is available for your distribution and kernel version. Otherwise, it will try to compile the driver locally. The script will also inform you if any required dependencies are missing (for example, if dkms or make is not present on your system).

If you want to install the eBPF probe instead, run:

```
$ falco-driver-loader bpf
```

Running Falco in a Container

The Falco Project provides several container images that you can use to run Falco in a container. Although the Falco container images described in this section will work with almost any container runtime, we'll use Docker in our examples for simplicity. If you want to use a different tool, including Kubernetes, you can apply the same concepts. Even if you are only interested in deploying Falco on Kubernetes, we still advise you to read this section as it presents some essential concepts.

Table 9-1 lists the main available images, which you can get from the Falco "Download" page (*https://oreil.ly/rkZoV*). These images contain all the necessary components to install the driver and run Falco. Later in this section, we'll discuss how to use them to support some common use cases.

Table 9-1. Falco container images hosted by the docker.io registry

Image name	Description
falcosecurity/ falco	This is the default Falco image. It contains Falco, the *falco-driver-loader* script, and the building toolchain (required to build the driver on the fly). The entry point of this image will call the *falco-driver-loader* script to automatically install the driver on the host before running Falco in the container.
falcosecurity/ falco-driver- loader	This image is similar to the default one, but it will not run Falco. The image entry point will only run the *falco-driver-loader* script. You can use it when you want to install the driver at a different moment or when using the principle of least privilege (see "Least privileged mode" on page 125). Since this image alone cannot run Falco, use it in combination with another image, like *falcosecurity/falco-no-driver*.
falcosecurity/ falco-no-driver	This alternative to the default image only contains Falco, so it cannot install the driver. Use it when using the principle of least privilege or when your data source does not need a driver (for example, when using a plugin).

Different tags are available for each distributed image. Tags allow you to choose a specific Falco version: for example, *falcosecurity/falco:0.32.0* contains Falco's 0.32.0 release. The *:latest* tag points to the latest released version of Falco.

If you want to experiment with a not-yet-released version of Falco, the *:master* tag ships the latest available development version. An automatic process builds and publishes images with this tag every time new code changes are merged into the master branch of Falco's GitHub repository. This means it is not a stable release—don't use it in production unless you want to try an experimental feature or debug a particular issue. Generally, we suggest always using the *:latest* tag, since it ships the latest Falco version and ruleset updates.

Next, we will describe how to use these images in the two common scenarios we've been discussing: syscall instrumentation, which requires a driver, and using a plugin as a data source, which does not.

Syscall Instrumentation Scenario

A Falco driver (either a kernel module or an eBPF probe) installed directly on the host is required for syscall instrumentation. Falco needs to run with enough privileges to interact with the driver; of course, if you want to use a container image to install the driver, that image needs to run with full privileges.

The Falco Project provides two modes for installing the driver on the fly and then running Falco in a container. The first and simplest mode uses just one container image with full privileges. The second uses two images: one image that temporarily runs with full privileges just to install the driver, and another image that then runs Falco with lesser privileges. The second approach allows enhanced security since the long-running container gets a restricted set of privileges, making life harder for a possible attacker. We recommend using least privileged mode to run Falco in a container.

Fully privileged mode

Running Falco in Docker with full privileges is quite straightforward. You just have to pull the default image:

```
$ docker pull falcosecurity/falco:latest
```

Then run Falco with the following command:

```
$ docker run --rm -i -t \
    --privileged \
    -v /var/run/docker.sock:/host/var/run/docker.sock \
    -v /dev:/host/dev \
    -v /proc:/host/proc:ro \
    -v /boot:/host/boot:ro \
    -v /lib/modules:/host/lib/modules:ro \
```

```
    -v /usr:/host/usr:ro \
    -v /etc:/host/etc:ro \
    falcosecurity/falco:latest
```

This command will install the driver on the fly before running Falco. The container image uses the kernel module by default. If you want to use the eBPF probe instead, just add the `-e FALCO_BPF_PROBE=""` option and remove `-v /dev:/host/dev` (only the kernel module requires *dev*).

As you can see, aside from the `--privileged` option, the preceding command mounts a set of paths from the host into the container (each `-v` option is a bind mount).

Specifically, the `-v /var/run/docker.sock:/host/var/run/docker.sock` option shares the Docker socket, so Falco can use Docker to obtain container metadata (as described in Chapter 5, where we discussed Falco's data enrichment techniques). You can add similar options for each container runtime available on your system. For example, if you also have containerd, include `-v /run/containerd/containerd.sock:/host/run/containerd/containerd.sock`.

Falco requires sharing *dev* and *proc* to interface with the driver and the system, respectively. Other shared paths are needed to install the driver.

Least privileged mode

This running mode follows the principle of least privilege (*https://oreil.ly/PKosx*) for enhanced security. Although this mode is the recommended way to run Falco in a container, it might not necessarily work for all systems and configurations. We advise you to give it a try anyway and fall back to the fully privileged mode only if this does not fit your environment.

As noted, this approach uses two different container images. The first step, which requires full privileges, is to install the driver using the *falcosecurity/falco-driver-loader* image. You'll need to do this before running Falco for the first time, and if you want to upgrade the driver at any point. (Alternatively, as explained earlier, you can install the driver directly on the host using the *falco-driver-loader* script shipped with the binary package. If you did so, skip this step.)

To install the driver using a container image, pull the image first:

```
$ docker pull falcosecurity/falco-driver-loader:latest
```

Then run the installation command:

```
$ docker run --rm -i -t \
    --privileged \
    -v /root/.falco:/root/.falco \
    -v /proc:/host/proc:ro \
    -v /boot:/host/boot:ro \
```

```
-v /lib/modules:/host/lib/modules:ro \
-v /usr:/host/usr:ro \
-v /etc:/host/etc:ro \
falcosecurity/falco-driver-loader:latest
```

This command installs the kernel module by default. If you want to use the eBPF probe instead, just add the -e `FALCO_BPF_PROBE=""` option.

The last step is to run Falco. Since the driver is already installed, you will just need to use the *falcosecurity/falco-no-driver* image. So, pull it first:

```
$ docker pull falcosecurity/falco-no-driver:latest
```

Then run Falco:

```
$ docker run --rm -i -t \
    -e HOST_ROOT=/ \
    --cap-add SYS_PTRACE --pid=host $(ls /dev/falco* | xargs -I {}
$ echo --device {}) \
    -v /var/run/docker.sock:/var/run/docker.sock \
    falcosecurity/falco-no-driver:latest
```

If you use another container runtime, customize this command by adding a -v option accordingly.

Finally, there are some caveats when using the eBPF probe. You cannot use least privileged mode unless you have at least kernel version 5.8. This is because, with previous kernel versions, loading the eBPF probe required the `--privileged` flag. If you are running a kernel version equal to or greater than 5.8, you can use the `SYS_BPF` capability to overcome this issue by customizing the command as follows:

```
$ docker run --rm -i -t \
    -e FALCO_BPF_PROBE="" \
    -e HOST_ROOT=/ \
    --cap-add SYS_PTRACE --cap-add SYS_BPF -pid=host \
    -v /root/.falco:/root/.falco \
    -v /var/run/docker.sock:/var/run/docker.sock \
    falcosecurity/falco-no-driver:latest
```

Note that on systems with the AppArmor Linux Security Module (LSM) enabled, you will also need to pass the following:

```
--security-opt apparmor:unconfined
```

 Depending on the Falco version you are using and your environment, you might need to customize the commands described in this section; refer to the online documentation (*https://oreil.ly/TXTge*).

Plugin Scenario

When you're using a plugin as your data source, there's no need to install a driver, nor will Falco need full privileges to run, so we recommend you use the *falcosecurity/ falco-no-driver* image for this scenario. Whatever container image you choose, the default Falco configuration it contains won't work out of the box; you'll have to give Falco the required configuration for the plugin. You can do that by using an external configuration file and mounting it in the container.

As a preparation step, you'll have to create a local copy of *falco.yaml* (*https://oreil.ly/ E31wy*) and modify it according to your plugin configuration. We will explain how to do that in the next chapter.

Once you've prepared your custom *falco.yaml*, to run Falco, use the following command:

```
$ docker run --rm -i -t \
    -v falco.yaml:/etc/falco/falco.yaml \
    falcosecurity/falco-no-driver:latest
```

If you want to use a plugin not shipped in the default Falco distribution, you will have to mount the plugin file and its rules file in the container, too. For example, to mount *libmyplugin.so* and *myplugin_rules.yaml*, add the following options to the preceding command:

```
-v /path/to/libmyplugin.so:/usr/share/falco/plugins/libmyplugin.so
-v /path/to/myplugin_rules.yaml:/etc/falco/myplugin_rules.yaml
```

Deploying to a Kubernetes Cluster

One of the most common Falco use cases is securing clusters, so deploying Falco to Kubernetes is perhaps the most important installation method to be aware of. The Falco Project recommends two approaches for this:

Helm
> The first installation method uses Helm, a very popular tool to install and manage software built for Kubernetes. The Falco community provides and maintains a Helm chart for Falco and other tools that integrate with Falco. Installing Falco using the provided chart is straightforward and mostly automatic.

Kubernetes manifest files
> The other installation method, geared toward flexibility, is based on a set of Kubernetes manifest files. These files provide default installation settings, which users can customize based on their needs. Although this approach requires a bit more effort, it permits the installation of Falco on virtually any Kubernetes cluster without the need for extra tools.

Both approaches are solid, and you should select the one that best suits your environment and your organization's requirements. In the following subsections, we will walk you through each of them. The only requirement is having a Kubernetes cluster installed and running.

 The installation methods for Kubernetes described in this section use the default Falco container image discussed in "Running Falco in a Container" on page 123.

Using Helm

If you prefer a fully automated installation process or are already using Helm in your environment, this installation method is for you. Having Helm (*https://helm.sh*) installed is a prerequisite; for instructions, see the online documentation (*https://oreil.ly/YCiLB*).

Falco's Helm chart will add Falco to all nodes in your cluster using a DaemonSet. Then each deployed Falco Pod will try to install the driver on its own node. That is the default configuration that reflects the most common scenario, syscall instrumentation.

 Falco Pods internally use *falco-driver-loader*, which tries to download a prebuilt driver; failing that, it will build the driver on the fly. Usually, no action is required. If you notice that the Falco Pods are continuously restarting after being deployed, the process was probably unable to install the driver. This issue usually happens when a prebuilt driver is unavailable for your distribution or kernel and no kernel headers are available on the host. To build the driver, kernel headers must be installed on the host. You can fix the issue by manually installing the kernel headers and then deploying Falco again.

Helm uses the Kubernetes context provided by kubectl (*https://oreil.ly/S7tqe*) to access your cluster. Before installing Falco with Helm, ensure that your local configuration points to the proper context. You can check that by running:

```
$ kubectl config current-context
```

If the context is not pointing to your targeted cluster or kubectl cannot access your cluster, you will have to address this issue. Otherwise, you can proceed with the next step.

Before installing the chart, add Falco's Helm repository so that your local Helm installation can find the Falco chart:

```
$ helm repo add falcosecurity https://falcosecurity.github.io/charts
```

Running this command is usually a one-time operation. To get the latest information about the Falco chart, use:

```
$ helm repo update
```

Execute this command whenever you want to install and update Falco with Helm.

The next and final step is actually to install the chart by running:

```
$ helm install falco falcosecurity/falco
```

The chart installs the kernel module by default. If you want to use the eBPF probe instead, just append `--set ebpf.enabled=true` to this command.

And you're done! After a while, Falco's Pods will show up in your cluster. You can use the following command to check whether they are ready:

```
$ kubectl get all
```

The chart installs Falco for the default scenario (syscall instrumentation), as per the default settings. The Helm installation process for other scenarios is very similar; just provide the appropriate configuration. We will discuss how to customize your Falco deployment in Chapter 10. You can find more information about Falco's chart configuration in its online documentation (*https://oreil.ly/pcJWP*).

Using Manifests

Kubernetes manifests are JSON or YAML files (mainly YAML) that contain the specifications for one or more Kubernetes API objects and describe your application and its configurations. The kubectl command-line utility lets you deploy your workload in Kubernetes using these files. Projects often provide almost-ready-to-use example manifests, but you'll usually need to adapt them to your needs.

Since Falco supports very different scenarios and environments, The Falco Project does not officially provide manifests for all use cases. However, for the syscall instrumentation scenario, you can use the Falco example manifests (*https://oreil.ly/qWW1w*) (listed in Table 9-2) as a starting point to make your customized manifests.[1]

---

[1] The actual URLs of the Falco manifest example files for Kubernetes may change from time to time, but you can always find links to them in the official documentation (*https://oreil.ly/P5BUa*). Falco's Helm chart can generate those files, too. Surprisingly, The Falco Project uses this Helm functionality to automatically publish up-to-date manifest example files under the Falcosecurity GitHub organization (*https://oreil.ly/6QhH3*).

Table 9-2. Example manifest files for Falco

Filename	Description
daemonset.yaml	Specifies a DaemonSet (*https://oreil.ly/9YwAV*) so that a copy of the Falco Pod will run on each node (required by the syscall instrumentation scenario). The Pod specification (*https://oreil.ly/WRtRb*) uses the *falcosecurity/falco* container image. It also includes all settings needed to run the image in this scenario, similar to those described in "Running Falco in a Container" on page 123.
configmap.yaml	Specifies a ConfigMap (*https://oreil.ly/vTAdd*) containing the default *falco.yaml* file and rules files. Modify it according to your needs.
serviceaccount.yaml	Specifies a ServiceAccount (*https://oreil.ly/sXkI9*) for running Falco's Pods. Falco requires this to talk with the Kubernetes API. You usually don't need to alter it, unless you want to change the service account name.
clusterrole.yaml	Specifies a ClusterRole (*https://oreil.ly/gWjN4*), including the role-based access control (RBAC) authorizations required by Falco to talk with the Kubernetes API. Don't change the list of permissions needed, or Falco will not enrich the Kubernetes metadata correctly.
clusterrolebinding.yaml	Specifies a ClusterRoleBinding (*https://oreil.ly/PTEcU*) that grants the permissions defined in *clusterrole.yaml* to the service account defined in *serviceaccount.yaml*. You usually won't need to change this, unless you've changed the service account or the cluster role name in the other files.

Once you've modified the manifest files according to your needs, to apply them to Kubernetes (that is, to deploy Falco to Kubernetes) just run the following command:

```
$ kubectl apply \
    -f ./templates/serviceaccount.yaml \
    -f ./templates/clusterrole.yaml \
    -f ./templates/clusterrolebinding.yaml \
    -f ./templates/configmap.yaml \
    -f ./templates/daemonset.yaml
```

Falco's Pods should show up in your cluster after a while. To check whether they are ready, use:

```
$ kubectl get all
```

If everything went well, Falco is now up and running in your production cluster—and you have learned how to customize your Falco deployment. Congratulations!

Conclusion

This chapter introduced the different installation methods available for Falco and explained the difference between the two most common installation scenarios. However, in some cases, your installation will need specific configurations or customizations. The next chapter gives you all the complementary information you need to finally run Falco in production and completely control your Falco installation.

Configuring and Running Falco

In the previous chapter, you learned how to install Falco in production environments. However, you still need to know how its configuration system works. Learning to change its settings is fundamental to managing them over time and accommodating your needs. You can configure Falco during or immediately after installation, when updating to a newer version, or any time your needs change.

This chapter will help you understand and use the available settings. First, we'll explain the main areas of intervention: command-line options, environment variables, the configuration file, and rules files. Then we will go deeper into each of them. You will also find valuable suggestions for production use cases, along with some tips to fine-tune your Falco configuration. At the end of the chapter you'll find a dedicated section on configuring plugins, and we'll show you how to update the configuration of a running Falco instance.

Configuring Falco

You can configure Falco through its settings, which we have grouped into three categories:

Command-line options and environment variables
Command-line options and environment variables are the first settings you need to run Falco. Most of these settings allow Falco to talk with your system, which is particularly important for system instrumentation and data enrichment. Other settings here let you adapt Falco to specific needs or help with troubleshooting.

Configuration file
You can configure almost any Falco behavior from within the main configuration file, which you can customize according to your needs. For instance, you can load rules files, activate the output channels you want, and use plugins if you

need to. By default Falco looks for this file at */etc/falco/falco.yaml*, but you can specify a different path using a command-line option.

Ruleset

Falco comes with a rich default ruleset so that you can start to use it immediately. However, the ruleset is perhaps the most critical aspect to customize. It represents the configuration of the Falco engine and sets what Falco will detect. By convention, rules files live in */etc/falco*.

Before we address each category in detail, we want to show you how Falco changes depending on how you install it.

Differences Among Installation Methods

Regardless of the installation method you choose, Falco's configuration areas will always be the same. However, the ways you can change the settings may be slightly different.

Host Installation

If you installed Falco using a package manager, you can specify the command-line options and environment variables directly in the systemd unit file, which you can find at */usr/lib/systemd/user/falco.service*. Using `systemctl edit falco` is a convenient way to do that. When you're finished, remember to restart the service with `systemctl restart falco`.

If you are not using a package manager, running Falco is entirely up to you, including passing command-line options and setting the environment variables. In such a case, you can manually create a systemd unit. You can use the *falco-service* file's source code (*https://oreil.ly/0LcF3*) as an example.

Regardless of the package you use, you'll find Falco's configuration and rules files under */etc/falco*. You can edit those files directly and then restart Falco.

Containers

Falco's container images allow you to specify the command to run, which by default is `/usr/bin/falco`. If you need to pass command-line options, do so through the CLI of your container runtime. For example, with Docker, to pass `--version`, you would use:

```
$ docker run --rm -it falcosecurity/falco /usr/bin/falco --version
```

Note that the *falcosecurity/falco* container image's entry point is a script that tries to install the driver automatically. If you want to skip the installation, you need to set the `SKIP_DRIVER_LOADER` environment variable to any nonempty value. In Docker, you can use the `-e` option to set an environment variable.[1] So, for example, to get the version and skip the driver installation at the same time, you would run:

```
$ docker run --rm -it -e SKIP_DRIVER_LOADER=y \
    falcosecurity/falco /usr/bin/falco --version
```

Falco container images also bundle both the default configuration file and the default rules files. If you need to modify any of these, the usual approach is to make an external copy of the file (for example, */etc/falco/falco.yaml*) and then mount it into the container. You can grab the configuration and rules files from the binary package (make sure it matches the version of Falco running in the container) and modify them according to your needs. Then, in Docker, use the `-v` option to mount the modified files into the container.[2]

Kubernetes Deployments

When you deploy Falco in Kubernetes, you'll also specify command-line options and environment variables in the DaemonSet or the Deployment manifest. If you use Helm or the example manifests from Chapter 9, the deployment will already be configured with all the options to connect to your container runtime and the Kubernetes API server. If you need to modify an option, find the corresponding Falco chart configuration (*https://oreil.ly/9CsSk*) or modify the manifest (*https://oreil.ly/L6rs9*) directly.

Another important difference is that configuration and rules files live inside a ConfigMap whose contents shadow those shipped within the container image. For Helm users, the maintainers update Falco's chart and configuration and rules files in sync with the Falco distribution. On the other hand, if you are using manifest files, it's completely up to you to ensure the ConfigMap embeds the right files.

Command-Line Options and Environment Variables

When running Falco, specifying a command-line option or setting an environment variable is sometimes the only way to change some of the settings. Settings you configure via the command line always take precedence over settings loaded from the configuration file.

---

1 There are several other ways to set environment variables when running a container in Docker; for more information, refer to Docker's online documentation (*https://oreil.ly/91H3j*).

2 There are several alternatives for mounting files into a container. For details, see Docker's documentation (*https://oreil.ly/4cdap*).

You can get the full list of Falco's command-line options by running `falco --help`. Falco will print each option (along with a brief description) in alphabetical order. The available options may change depending on the Falco version. Always refer to `falco --help` when in doubt.

In the rest of this section, to help familiarize you with the most important settings, we group them by function. We also provide detailed information about using environment variables, which you will not find in `falco --help`.

Configuration Settings

The two command-line options shown in Table 10-1 pertain to Falco's configuration file (located by default at */etc/falco/falco.yaml*). The first one allows you to load a configuration file from a different location; the second allows you to override some configuration values on the fly. You won't usually need to use them, but they can be handy when troubleshooting. Also, when running Falco in production, ensure nobody sets them by mistake so that Falco uses the correct configuration file and the intended settings.

Table 10-1. Configuration command-line options

Option	Description
-c	Sets the path to the configuration file Falco will load. If this is not set, Falco uses the default path: */etc/falco/falco.yaml*.
-o, --option <key>=<val>	Overrides a value in the configuration file by setting the value <val> to the configuration option specified by <key>. You can use dot notation (.) to specify nested options or square brackets notation ([ ]) to access lists: for example, -o key.subkey.list[0]=myValue.

Instrumentation Settings (Syscalls Only)

As you learned in Chapters 4 and 9, Falco uses the kernel module driver by default. You can switch to the eBPF probe by setting the FALCO_BPF_PROBE environment variable. You can set it to the path of the probe you want to use: for example, FALCO_BPF_PROBE="/path/to/falco-bpf.o". Otherwise, you can set it to an empty string (FALCO_BPF_PROBE="") and Falco will use *~/.falco/falco-bpf.o* by default.

When you run Falco in a container or Kubernetes, the container image supports FALCO_BPF_PROBE to control the on-the-fly driver installation, along with other environment variables. (The *falco-driver-loader* script exposes most of them, so you can also use `falco-driver-loader --help` to get more information.) Let's look at those environment variables now:

DRIVERS_REPO

If you create a repository of prebuilt drivers (either kernel modules or eBPF probes), you can use this option to instruct the script to download a driver from your repository. A driver repository hosts files with the following URL structure:

<DRIVERS_REPO>/<DRIVER_VERSION>/falco_<OS_ID>
_<KERNEL_RELEASE>_<KERNEL_VERSION>.[ko|o]

This variable allows you to set the base URL of your repository (with no trailing slash). You may want to use this setting if you are running Falco in an air-gapped environment or if you don't want to download prebuilt drivers from the internet. If not set, this variable defaults to The Falco Project's public driver repository (*https://oreil.ly/vsE8X*).

DRIVER_INSECURE_DOWNLOAD

If your driver repository does not support HTTPS, set it to any value (for example, yes) to allow the script to download files from insecure URLs.

SKIP_DRIVER_LOADER

If you installed the driver on the host by other means, you'll likely want to disable the *falco-driver-loader* script when the container starts. In that case, set this environment variable to any value (for example, yes). This setting only affects Falco container images that use *falco-driver-loader* in the entry point, like the *falcosecurity/falco* container image.

HOST_ROOT

This environment variable differs from the others listed here in that it's not related to the driver installation and directly affects Falco. HOST_ROOT expects a base path and affects the instrumentation setup and enrichment system. If the value is not empty, Falco uses it as a path prefix when it accesses the host's filesystem to use the kernel module devices (under */dev*) or to fetch information for data enrichment (in particular from */proc* and the container runtime Unix socket path). The *falco-driver-loader* script uses this variable for similar purposes (for example, to access */boot*, */lib*, */usr*, and */etc*).

Use HOST_ROOT when running Falco in a container. The usual convention is to set HOST_ROOT=/host and mount all the relevant paths into the container under the */host* directory. Kubernetes deployment uses this approach; see Chapters 5 and 9 for more details.

For completeness, other settings related to syscall instrumentation are listed in Table 10-2. These settings have a significant performance impact, so don't use them unless you need to.

Table 10-2. Syscall instrumentation command-line options

Option	Description
-A	Falco does not monitor all syscalls by default, so you usually cannot use all event types in rule conditions (the driver skips most syscalls that are noisy or expensive to process, such as read, write, send, and recv). If you enable this setting, the driver will send all supported syscall events to Falco, which may be helpful in edge use cases. However, enabling this setting has a severe performance penalty. Falco may not be able to catch up with the event stream. The full list of supported syscalls is available in *syscall_info_table.c* (*https://oreil.ly/WVDRm*). By default, the driver skips those marked with EF_DROP_SIMPLE_CONS.
-u, --userspace	Use this option only when you can't use the kernel space instrumentation. This option must be used with a user-space driver like pdig (discussed in Chapter 4).

Data Enrichment Settings (Syscalls Only)

When using syscalls as a data source, Falco needs to connect to a driver. It also needs to fetch information from the host, the container runtime, and Kubernetes. In Chapter 5, we talked briefly about the settings described in this section; Table 10-3 provides detailed usage descriptions of command-line options and environment variables that affect the data enrichment mechanism.

Table 10-3. Data enrichment command-line options

Option	Description
--cri <path>	Use this option to specify the path to the Unix socket of a CRI-compatible container runtime. If the Unix socket is valid, Falco will connect to the runtime to fetch the container metadata. In recent versions of Falco, you can specify this option multiple times. Falco will try each given path in order and use the first one that connects. When this option is not set, Falco will only try to use */run/containerd/containerd.sock*.
--disable-cri-async	This option disables asynchronous CRI metadata fetching. You won't usually need to set it. However, if Falco shows container metadata intermittently, this option can help you fix the issue.
-k <url>, --k8s-api <url>	This enables Kubernetes metadata enrichment by connecting to the Kubernetes API server specified by <url>. Alternatively, you can use the FALCO_K8S_API environment variable, which accepts the same values allowed by this option.

Option	Description
`-K <bt_file>` | `<cert_file>:<key_file[#pwd]>` `[:<ca_cert_file>]`, `--k8s-api-cert <bt_file>` | `<cert_file>:<key_file[#pwd]>` `[:<ca_cert_file>]`	Use this option to authenticate with the Kubernetes API server. You can provide either a bearer token file[a] (`<bt_file>`) or a certificate and a private key (`<cert_file>:<key_file>`). If you use the latter, you can optionally use a passphrase (`#pwd`) to access the private key, if encrypted, and a CA certificate (`:<ca_cert_file>`) to verify the API server's identity. Certificates and private keys must be provided in the PEM file format. As an alternative, you can use the `FALCO_K8S_API_CERT` environment variable, which accepts the same values allowed by this option.
`--k8s-node <node_name>`	This option enables an important performance optimization for Kubernetes metadata enrichment: Falco will use the node name as a filter when requesting metadata of Pods from the API server, discarding unnecessary metadata coming from other nodes. You should always set this option. If you don't, Falco will work, but may have performance issues on large clusters.

[a] A bearer token file contains a string that authenticates the API request, one of the available authentication strategies (*https://oreil.ly/nh9Qk*) for Kubernetes.

Ruleset Settings

Table 10-4 shows the command-line options that can affect the ruleset. Falco will only use the configuration file to load rules if you don't use any of these options.

Table 10-4. Ruleset command-line options

Option	Description
`-D <substring>`	This option allows you to disable one or more rules that match `<substring>` in their names. You can specify it multiple times, but it is incompatible with the `-t` option (see below).
`-r <rules_file>`	This option allows you to specify a file or a directory that Falco will use to load rules. In the case of a directory, Falco loads all the files it contains. You can specify `-r` multiple times to load multiple files or directories. If you use this option, Falco will ignore any rules files and directories specified in the configuration file (*/etc/falco/falco.yaml*). Thus, we do not recommend using it in production, except for debugging or in special cases.
`-T <tag>`	This option disables any rules with the given `<tag>`. You can specify it multiple times, but it is incompatible with the `-t` option (see below).
`-t <tag>`	This option enables only rules with the given `<tag>` and disables all others. You can specify it multiple times, but it is incompatible with the `-T` and `-D` options.

Output Settings

We described most of the output formatting options (along with Falco output channel configuration) in Chapter 8. However, two other command-line options (listed in Table 10-5) allow you to further customize Falco's output behavior.

Table 10-5. Output command-line options

Option	Description
-p*<output_format>*, --print*<output_format>*	When enabled, this option appends additional information to the Falco notification's output. A few flavors are available; for instance: • -pc or -pcontainer will add container information, such as the name and ID. • -pk or -pkubernetes will add Kubernetes information, such as the namespace and Pod name. We recommend using -pk when using Falco in a Kubernetes context.
-U, --unbuffered	This option disables full output buffering in the output channels (see Chapter 8). Use it only if you encounter issues when piping the Falco output into another process or script. Turning off output buffering may increase CPU usage.

Other Settings for Debugging and Troubleshooting

The command-line options we have described so far are the ones you're likely to use routinely while operating Falco. However, there's another group of options (listed in Table 10-6) for more occasional use, such as when you need information about your Falco installation or are trying to solve a problem.

Table 10-6. Command-line options for debugging and troubleshooting

Option	Description
-e *<events_file>*	Tells Falco to use the trace file (see Chapter 3) specified by *<events_file>* as a data source instead of using a live event source. Once Falco consumes all the events in the file, it exits. Useful for testing and rule authoring.
-L	Prints information about all loaded rules.
-l *<rule>*	Prints the name and description of the rule with name *<rule>*, if loaded.
--list[=*<source>*]	Lists all available condition fields, grouped by class (see Chapter 6). If you also provide *<source>*, Falco will only list fields for that data source. The value of *<source>* can be syscall or any other data source provided by configured plugins.
--list-plugins	Prints information about configured plugins.
-s *<stats_file>*	Tells Falco to create the file *<stats_file>* and populate it with statistics while running.
--stats-interval *<msec>*	Sets the refresh interval (in milliseconds) for updating the file created by -s *<stats_file>*.
--support	Prints details about the loaded Falco configuration and ruleset, and other useful information for troubleshooting that you can provide when asking for help (for example, when opening an issue (*https://oreil.ly/vkk2h*) in the Falco GitHub repository).
-V, --validate *<rules_file>*	Validates the content of the given *<rules_file>*. Useful for testing and rule authoring.
-v	Enables verbose logging while Falco is running. This option does not affect the usual Falco notifications, but log messages may interleave. Useful for debugging.
--version	Prints the version of Falco you are using.

Configuration File

We talk about Falco's configuration file all throughout this book, and we've already covered its most important aspects. This section provides an overview and pointers to everything you may need.

The configuration file is a YAML file, located at */etc/falco/falco.yaml* by default. In this file, you can configure:

Rules files
> The `rules_file` configuration node is the first one you'll find in the configuration file. It allows you to choose which rules files Falco will load (more on these in the next section).

Plugins
> You can enable plugins and pass settings through the `load_plugins` and `plugins` configuration nodes (see "Using Plugins" on page 142).

Output channels
> Various configuration nodes allow you to configure formatting, logging, and output channel options. Refer to Chapter 8 for more information on the output framework.

Embedded servers
> Falco provides an embedded web server that exposes a healthy endpoint.[3] Container orchestrators and other applications can use this endpoint to check if Falco is up and running. The `webserver` configuration node allows you to enable and configure the server.
>
> Falco also provides a gRPC server that you can enable and configure using the `grpc` configuration node (see Chapters 8 and 12).

Advanced fine-tuning settings (syscalls only)
> Syscall instrumentation is likely the most complex feature Falco supports, so the configuration file also provides advanced settings for it. Those settings vary between versions of Falco, so we suggest you always refer to the online documentation and the inline comments included in the configuration file.
>
> Notable options here include `syscall_event_drops`, which controls the detection of dropped events; `syscall_event_timeouts`, which helps detect the absence of events (an uncommon situation for syscalls); and `metadata_download`,

---

3 Falco's developers initially introduced the web server to support the Kubernetes audit log as a data source. Recently, they factored out this functionality into a plugin. Thus, the actual settings you can find under the `webserver` configuration node may vary significantly from one Falco version to another.

which provides several options to fine-tune information downloads from the container orchestrator API server.

Ruleset

Falco comes with a set of predefined rules that you can use right out of the box. However, there are good reasons to customize your ruleset as much as possible. The default ruleset is designed to cover major attack vectors, but these rules cannot cover all possible cases. Attack mechanisms are always evolving, so your ruleset needs to keep up. If you want the highest level of security, you need a ruleset that's tailored to your specific environment.

Additional benefits of customizing your rules include avoiding noisy false positives and optimizing Falco's performance. You need to learn how to configure the ruleset correctly for all of these reasons.

Loading Rules Files

There are two ways to tell Falco which rules files to load: through the command line or the configuration file. On the command line, you specify rules files using the -r flag. In the configuration file, you put rules files under the `rules_file` section. Recall that anything you set via the command line will take precedence over the configuration file. In production, we recommend loading rules files through the configuration file *only*, for this reason.

Whichever method you choose, you can specify more than one rules file or directory. So, you can do:

```
$ falco -r path/to/my/rulefile1.yaml -r path/to/my/rulefile2.yaml
```

or:

```
rules_file:
  - path/to/my/rulefile1.yaml
  - path/to/my/rulefile2.yaml
```

It's important to be aware that rules files are loaded and parsed in the order you specify. (When the entry is a directory, Falco will load every file in that directory in alphabetical order.) This makes it possible to customize rules, macros, and lists (see Chapter 7) that are defined in one file in a subsequent file. The default Falco configuration is crafted to take advantage of this mechanism.

Let's take a look at the `rules_file` section in the default configuration file that is shipped with Falco:

```
rules_file:
  - /etc/falco/falco_rules.yaml
  - /etc/falco/falco_rules.local.yaml
  - /etc/falco/rules.d
```

The main rules file, *falco_rules.yaml*, which contains rules for syscalls, is followed by a file named *falco_rules.local.yaml*. This file is where you should make changes to *falco_rules.yaml*. It is empty by default, and you can work in it without having to worry about polluting the main rules file. You can create other local files as you need.

Usually, Falco provides one rules file per data source. You can use this approach or use multiple files, depending on your needs. Just keep in mind that the loading order matters. Also note that Falco will only load rules that match the configured data source; all others will be ignored. This means you don't have to worry about manually removing or disabling rules files intended for other data sources.

Tuning the Ruleset

The most important aspect of tuning the ruleset is understanding what your use case needs to detect. That will allow you to decide which rules work for you and which do not. Avoiding unnecessary rules has the double benefit of increasing performance (Falco will use less CPU resources) and reducing false positives.

Once you have done an initial skim, disable the rules you are not interested in (as described in Chapter 7). We do not suggest removing them from the rules files unless you have created your own rules files from scratch. We also recommend periodically evaluating your ruleset, because the rules you need will change over time.

Next, look at the rules' conditions. We'll get into the details of writing Falco rules in Chapter 13, but for now we'll offer two general guidelines for evaluating Falco rules.

First, *avoid using too many exceptions in conditions*: for example, long chains of and not (...) and not (...). Falco has no alternative but to sequentially check any exception present in the condition, which is an expensive task. Shorter conditions, whenever possible, can improve rule evaluation performance significantly.

The second guideline applies only to syscalls and holds that *a rule condition should always match just one event type or a small set of event types*. For example, evt.type=connect and evt.type in (open,openat,openat2) are both fine, but evt.type!=execve is not, because that filter would match all event types except one, which is too many. Falco indexes rules by event type as a way of optimizing its internal evaluation process; a rule matching too many event types would make this indexing inefficient. To help rule authors spot this issue, Falco emits warnings for rules that match all event types.

Using Plugins

By default, Falco comes configured to use syscalls. If you want to use a plugin as your data source instead, make sure that:

- The plugin file is already available in */usr/share/falco/plugins* (some plugins are shipped with Falco); if not, you'll need to install it in that folder.
- A rules file for the plugin is available (we recommend placing it under */etc/falco*).
- You have read the plugin's documentation and understand which configuration parameters it needs.

Then, preparing Falco's configuration file to use a plugin is a three-step process: select the correct rules file, configure the plugin, and enable it.

To illustrate this process, we will use the CloudTrail plugin (*https://oreil.ly/kgImn*), which fetches log files containing CloudTrail (*https://oreil.ly/DUEDJ*) events (details on using this plugin are provided in the next chapter). The CloudTrail plugin has a ruleset that requires another plugin with field extraction capability: the JSON plugin (*https://oreil.ly/Viiaj*). Both plugins and the ruleset come bundled with Falco out of the box, so you should already have them if you've installed Falco. You'll find the plugin files *libcloudtrail.so* and *libjson.so* under */usr/share/falco/plugins* and the rules file at */etc/falco/aws_cloudtrail_rules.yaml*.

Rules files for plugins are not usually configured by default in the Falco configuration, so you'll have to add an entry to `rules_file` to load the correct rules file (you can also remove unnecessary ones if you want to):

```
rules_file:
  - /etc/falco/aws_cloudtrail_rules.yaml
```

Next, under `plugins`, add the relevant entries:

```
plugins:
  - name: cloudtrail
    library_path: libcloudtrail.so
    init_config:
      sqsDelete: true
    open_params: "sqs://my-sqs-queue"
  - name: json
    library_path: libjson.so
    init_config: ""
```

The `name` field must match the plugin name, and `library_path` must match the plugin file under */usr/share/falco/plugins*.

In `init_config`, add the initialization parameters that Falco will pass to the plugin (refer to your plugin's documentation for details). Most plugins accept either a plaintext or a JSON-formatted string. If the plugin supports a JSON string, you can still use the YAML syntax for `init_config` (as in the preceding example); Falco will automatically convert it for you.

The `open_params` setting is needed only for plugins with event sourcing capability (such as the CloudTrail plugin) and accepts only a plain-text string. It provides the parameters to open the stream of events (again, refer to your plugin's documentation). Some plugins might not need this setting; in that case, you can just set it to an empty string (`""`).

The last step is to enable your plugins:

```
load_plugins: [cloudtrail, json]
```

The `load_plugins` setting accepts an array of plugin names. You can enable multiple plugins at the same time.[4]

That's it! Your plugins are now configured and ready to run in Falco.

Changing the Configuration

Once you've installed and configured Falco, you may need to change its configuration from time to time. There are two ways to tell Falco to load an updated configuration (that is, any modification to the configuration file or rules files).

The simplest method is just to modify the configuration and then restart Falco. If you installed Falco on the host using a package manager, you can do this with `systemctl restart falco`. If you are running Falco in a container, restart the container. If you're running it in a Kubernetes cluster, you'll need to redeploy Falco. Restarting Falco is the only way to upgrade to a newer version or change its command-line settings.

The second way to load an updated configuration is to *hot-reload*, or tell Falco to reload the configuration and rules files without stopping its running process. You can tell Falco to reload itself by sending a SIGHUP signal (*https://oreil.ly/6unav*):

```
$ kill -HUP <falco process ID here>
```

Once Falco receives the signal, it will reload the configuration file and the configured rules files.

Since version 0.32.0, Falco can automatically hot-reload when the configuration file or a rules file is modified. In the configuration file, the `watch_config_files` setting controls this feature (enabled by default). So, in recent versions of Falco, you can just

---

4 The first versions of Falco with the plugin system do not allow you to enable multiple plugins with the event sourcing capability at the same time. However, you can enable multiple plugins with only the field extraction capability (see Chapter 4).

change the configuration file or rules files without the need to send a SIGHUP signal manually.

Note that when Falco is restarting or hot reloading, it does not detect events. However, the amount of time required to hot-reload Falco is significantly shorter than the time it takes to restart the process, and is usually negligible.

Conclusion

This chapter and the previous one provided in-depth coverage of installing, configuring, and running Falco in a production environment, for both the syscall instrumentation scenario and the scenario where you're using a plugin as a data source. Now, it's time to dig deeper into a concrete plugin case: using Falco for cloud security. In the next chapter, you will discover how to secure your cloud by taking advantage of the CloudTrail plugin.

CHAPTER 11

Using Falco for Cloud Security

Now that you've learned all you need to know about configuring and running Falco, it's time to focus on an important topic that can have a huge impact on your security posture: cloud security.

If you are reading this book, there is a good chance that some of your software (or all of it!) runs in the cloud. Since AWS is the leading provider of cloud services, there is also a good chance that your software is running there.

Public clouds are great environments to run software. Their support for elasticity, flexibility, and automation makes building and running apps easier and more efficient. However, cloud-based apps and the data they use are exposed to attacks from the whole planet. They are also exposed to misconfigurations, mistakes, and malicious behavior from internal teams.

A comprehensive security posture needs to take many domains into account, including applications, users (external and internal), and data. Failing to properly protect any one of these domains will result in gaps and therefore in risk. For example, protecting workloads that run in containers and hosts (which you can do effectively with Falco) is not beneficial unless you also cover the cloud infrastructure where these workloads run.

Fortunately, Falco can bridge this gap and help you achieve the coverage you need. Let's learn how!

Why Falco for AWS Security?

Cloud security is a fertile and constantly evolving space with many implementation options. Architecturally, most of those options fall into two basic categories:

1. Tools that query cloud APIs or watch cloud data stores to detect misconfigurations or vulnerabilities

2. Tools that stream cloud logs into a backend, index them, and let you query them

If your goal is to detect threats in cloud-based software, tools in category 1 won't be very useful. Polling is great for detecting gaps and validating compliance, but lacks the real-time nature required to detect threats and respond quickly. Category 2 tools are powerful, but also tremendously expensive (especially in environments like the public cloud, where tons of logs are produced) and not friendly to deploy and use.

The Falco runtime security approach provides a very effective solution to this problem. Falco's philosophy is based on three key concepts. First, it parses data in a streaming fashion to detect threats in real time. Second, it implements detection on top of an engine that is lightweight to run and easy to deploy. Third, it offers a compact rule language that is quick to learn but flexible and expressive. This philosophy, as you've seen throughout the book, is very effective with system calls and works equally well when applied to logs like those produced by AWS CloudTrail.

Falco consumes few resources and, most importantly, analyzes the data in a streaming way—no need to perform expensive copies or wait until the data is indexed. Falco looks at your data in real time and notifies you of problems in seconds. Getting it up and running takes only a few minutes, as you saw in Part I of this book, and adopting it for both cloud logs and system calls allows a unified approach to threat detection. Let's look at how it works.

Falco's Architecture and AWS Security

When deployed in the context of AWS infrastructure security, Falco implements detections on top of a specific data source: the logs generated by AWS CloudTrail. The way this works is shown in Figure 11-1.

Figure 11-1. The high-level architecture of a Falco deployment for AWS security

CloudTrail is a log aggregation service offered by Amazon. It collects logs from hundreds of AWS services and stores them in S3, using a consistent and well-documented format. CloudTrail is easy to set up and offers a coherent layer that insulates the customer from the complexities of collecting logs of users' and services' activity.

CloudTrail events are entries in JSON files that CloudTrail writes in the S3 bucket at regular intervals. Falco understands how to read and parse these events thanks to the CloudTrail plugin (Figure 11-2), which is created and maintained by the Falco community. (If you need a refresher on what Falco plugins are and how they work, see Chapter 4.)

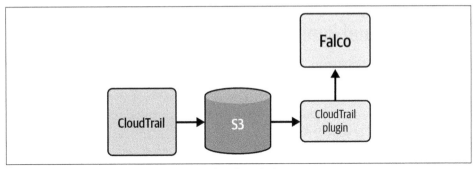

Figure 11-2. Event collection with the CloudTrail plugin

In addition to offering multiple methods to collect CloudTrail logs (more on each of these methods later in the chapter), the CloudTrail plugin extends Falco with AWS-specific fields, which you can use to create rules like this one:

```
- rule: Console Login Without MFA
  desc: Detect a console login without MFA.
  condition: >
    ct.name="ConsoleLogin" and ct.error=""
    and ct.user.identitytype!="AssumedRole"
    and json.value[/responseElements/ConsoleLogin]="Success"
    and json.value[/additionalEventData/MFAUsed]="No"
  output: >
    Detected a console login without MFA
    (requesting user=%ct.user, requesting IP=%ct.srcip, AWS region=%ct.region)
  priority: CRITICAL
  source: aws_cloudtrail
```

Once Falco's CloudTrail plugin is configured with a CloudTrail trail as an input, Falco will continuously analyze the trail's upcoming data, providing real-time anomaly and threat detection. It's like having a security camera for your cloud activity!

Detection Examples

Here are some of the things you can detect with Falco when it's configured for AWS security:

- Someone logs into the AWS console without multifactor authentication (MFA).
- Someone deactivates MFA for the root user.
- Someone creates a new AWS user or group.

- Someone runs instances in a nonapproved region.
- Someone changes the permissions of an S3 bucket.
- Someone disables CloudTrail logging.

For the full list, refer to the CloudTrail rules file (*https://oreil.ly/beQYF*).

Configuring and Running Falco for CloudTrail Security

This part of the chapter will outline approaches to setting up cloud security using Falco, describe the components, and guide you through configuring everything properly. As we mentioned, Falco's integration with CloudTrail happens through the CloudTrail plugin (*https://oreil.ly/OWVgb*). The plugin can be configured to receive log files in three different ways:

- A Simple Queue Service (SQS) queue that passes along Simple Notification Service (SNS) notifications about new log files
- An S3 bucket
- A local filesystem path

Of these three methods, the first one is what you will use in the vast majority of production situations, so we will focus on it first.

Receiving Log Files Through an SQS Queue

This deployment method consists of leveraging SQS to notify Falco when new Cloud-Trail logs are produced. Falco monitors the SQS queue and parses new logs in real time when they arrive. The process is depicted in Figure 11-3.

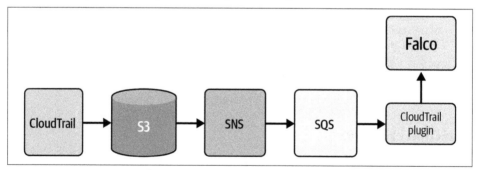

Figure 11-3. SQS queue collection diagram

The process of setting up Falco in this configuration involves three steps:

1. Creating the CloudTrail trail and configuring it with an SNS topic. The SNS topic detects changes to the S3 bucket where the trail is depositing the files and broadcasts them to the world.

2. Creating the SQS queue and attaching it to the SNS topic. This creates an endpoint that Falco can use to detect the arrival of new data.

3. Configuring Falco to receive the logs using the SQS queue.

We will guide you with step-by-step instructions to set all of this up, so you have full knowledge of the moving parts. Before doing that, however, we'll show you the easy shortcut: a Terraform module that will do the work for you.

Terraform-based deployment

You can find the Terraform module on GitHub (*https://oreil.ly/4qvQX*). Clone the repository to your local machine and then execute the following commands:

```
$ cd examples/single-account
$ terraform init
$ terraform validate
$ terraform apply
```

If all goes well, you should get output that looks like this:

```
Apply complete! Resources: 14 added, 0 changed, 0 destroyed.

Outputs:

cloudtrail_sns_subscribed_sqs_arn = "arn:aws:sqs:ZZZZ"
cloudtrail_sns_subscribed_sqs_url = "https://sqs.<REGION>.amazonaws.com/.../
<QUEUE_NAME>"
```

You can now use *<QUEUE_NAME>* in your *falco.yaml* file:

```
plugins:
  - name: cloudtrail
    library_path: libcloudtrail.so
    init_config: ""
    open_params: "sqs://<QUEUE_NAME>"
  - name: json
    library_path: libjson.so
    init_config: ""
load_plugins: [cloudtrail, json]
```

Next, configure the `rules_file` section of *falco.yaml* to load the CloudTrail rules:

```
rules_file:
  - /etc/falco/aws_cloudtrail_rules.yaml
```

and you're ready to launch Falco!

Manual deployment

Here are the steps to follow to set up Falco with an SQS queue if you don't want to use the Terraform script. The first step is to create the trail. You can do this as follows:

1. Go to the CloudTrail section of the AWS console.
2. Click "Create trail."
3. Name the trail *Falco*.
4. As the storage location, you can either pick an existing trail or tell AWS to create a new one.
5. Uncheck "Log file SSE-KMS encryption." SSE encryption is something you should definitely use as a good practice, but configuring it goes beyond the scope of this chapter.
6. Check "SNS notification delivery."
7. Under "Create a new SNS topic," select New and name the topic *falco-cloudtrail-logs*.
8. Click Next.
9. The "Choose log events" page lets you pick which logs you want to capture. The default settings are enough for Falco to operate properly. Checking "Data events" or "Exclude Amazon RDS Data API events" will allow you, if you desire, to craft more granular rules on data events, like S3 bucket-level and object-level access.
10. Click Next.
11. Click "Create trail."

Next, create the SQS queue:

1. Go to the SQS section of the AWS console.
2. Click "Create queue."
3. Name the queue *falco-queue*.
4. The default access policy will work as is with Falco. However, consider implementing a less privileged access policy, for example using the AWS Policy Generator (*https://oreil.ly/fyxDD*).
5. Click "Create queue" at the bottom of the page. This will bring you to the *falco-queue* details page.
6. Click "Subscribe to Amazon SNS topic."
7. Select the topic whose name ends in *falco-cloudtrail-logs*.
8. Click Save.

Now you need to configure Falco. This involves setting up AWS authentication and configuring Falco itself. To read log files from an S3 bucket or SNS notifications from an SQS queue Falco needs authentication credentials, and it needs to be configured with an AWS region. Falco relies on the same authentication mechanisms used by the AWS Go SDK (*https://oreil.ly/DmUSL*): environment variables or shared configuration files. Configure these as follows:

Environment variables

Specify the AWS region with `AWS_REGION=xxx`, the access key ID with `AWS_ACCESS_KEY_ID=xxx`, and the secret key with `AWS_SECRET_ACCESS_KEY=xxx`. Here's a sample command line:

```
AWS_DEFAULT_REGION=us-west-1 \
AWS_ACCESS_KEY_ID=xxx \
AWS_SECRET_ACCESS_KEY=xxx \
falco -c <path-to-falco.yaml> -r <path-to-falco-rules>
```

Shared configuration files

Specify the AWS region in a file at *$HOME/.aws/config* and the credentials in a file at *$HOME/.aws/credentials*. Here are some examples of what these files will look like:

```
$HOME/.aws/config
[default]
region = us-west-1

$HOME/.aws/credentials
[default]
aws_access_key_id=<YOUR-AWS-ACCESS-KEY-ID-HERE>
aws_secret_access_key=<YOUR-AWS-SECRET-ACCESS-KEY-HERE>
```

Now, set up Falco itself:

1. Add the following snippet to *falco.yaml* to configure SQS-based log collection:

```
plugins:
  - name: cloudtrail
    library_path: libcloudtrail.so
    init_config: ""
    open_params: "sqs://falco-queue"
  - name: json
    library_path: libjson.so
    init_config: ""
load_plugins: [cloudtrail, json]
```

2. Configure the `rules_file` section of *falco.yaml* to load the CloudTrail rules:

```
rules_file:
  - /etc/falco/aws_cloudtrail_rules.yaml
```

3. Start Falco.

Et voilà: your AWS infrastructure is now protected!

Reading Events from an S3 Bucket or the Local Filesystem

While the SQS-based setup is recommended for real-time detection, Falco can also read CloudTrail logs directly from the S3 bucket or from a copy of the logs stored in the local filesystem. While the SQS setup processes "live" logs as they arrive, the S3 and local filesystem setups read stored data. This means they effectively operate in the past and cause Falco to exit when they reach the end of the currently stored data. This approach can be valuable for a couple of reasons. First, it allows you to iterate quickly during rule development. Second, it allows you to run Falco "back in time" on CloudTrail logs that have already been stored (even if they've been stored for a long time). Curious if (or when) somebody has changed the permissions of a bucket during the last three weeks? Point Falco to the logs and you can find out easily!

Let's take a look at how to run Falco in this mode.

S3 bucket

First, you need to set up AWS authentication. We just described how to do this for SQS access, and it works exactly the same for S3, so just go back and follow the steps at the end of the previous section.

Once you've configured AWS authentication, add the following snippet to *falco.yaml*:

```
plugins:
  - name: cloudtrail
    library_path: libcloudtrail.so
    init_config:
    s3DownloadConcurrency: 64
    open_params: >
        s3://my-s3-bucket/AWSLogs/411571310278/CloudTrail/us-west-1/2021/09/23/
  - name: json
    library_path: libjson.so
    init_config: ""
    load_plugins: [cloudtrail, json]
```

Note how the open_params key is just the URI of the trail location on S3, which you can easily obtain by navigating to the data in the S3 console and then clicking "Copy S3 URI." You don't need to specify the whole bucket; you can point to a subdirectory or even a specific log file.

Now you need to configure the rules_file section of *falco.yaml* to load the Cloud-Trail rules:

```
rules_file:
  - /etc/falco/aws_cloudtrail_rules.yaml
```

After that, you can just run Falco. It will process every file below the provided S3 URI and return when it's done.

Parsing the logs from a machine outside AWS, such as your laptop, might be pretty slow, because the machine needs to download the data in order to process it. You can speed things up by increasing the download concurrency (`s3DownloadConcurrency` in the `init_config` key), or predownload the data locally using the AWS CLI and then point Falco to the local logs (which we'll describe next).

Local filesystem path

You can process CloudTrail logs stored in the local filesystem by putting the following configuration in *falco.yaml*:

```
plugins:
  - name: cloudtrail
    library_path: libcloudtrail.so
    init_config: ""
    open_params: >
        /home/user/cloudtrail-logs/059797578166_CloudTrail_us-east-1_2021...
  - name: json
    library_path: libjson.so
    init_config: ""
    load_plugins: [cloudtrail, json]
```

You can point to a single file or to a directory, in which case Falco will recursively read all of the files in the directory.

You will also need to edit the `rules_file` section of *falco.yaml* to load the CloudTrail rules:

```
rules_file:
  - /etc/falco/aws_cloudtrail_rules.yaml
```

Once you've done that, just run Falco. It will process all of the files and exit when it's done.

Extending Falco's AWS Ruleset

Falco comes with a powerful set of CloudTrail-based rules. However, if you need customization, the CloudTrail plugin exports a rich set of fields that you can use to craft your own rules with a high level of granularity.

Writing Falco rules will be extensively covered in Chapter 13. However, since that chapter is primarily focused on system call–based rules, here are a couple of tips that will help you get started with cloud rules development:

- CloudTrail rules need to include the following key: `source: aws_cloudtrail`. This tells Falco that the fields in the rule condition and output must come from the CloudTrail plugin.

- You can obtain a list of fields you can use in a CloudTrail rule by using the `--list=aws_cloudtrail` Falco command-line switch. Also, take a look at Table 6-10 in Chapter 6.

What About Other Clouds?

AWS is a very important player in cloud computing, so Falco added support for it first. However, at the time of writing the Falco community was working on adding support for both Microsoft Azure and Google Cloud Platform. Expect more clouds to be added in the long term!

If you want to find out if Falco supports your cloud, check out the plugins repository on GitHub (*https://oreil.ly/W20tv*).

Conclusion

In this chapter, you learned that Falco is about more than system calls and containers, and how you can employ it to protect your cloud software and vastly improve your security posture. In the next chapter we will switch to the output side and show you how to collect and treat Falco events.

CHAPTER 12

Consuming Falco Events

At this point, you've learned how to run and configure Falco. You understand how Falco can be used for runtime and cloud security and how it can detect a vast spectrum of threats. Now, it's time to focus on what you can do with Falco's detections. Consuming Falco's output is the final piece of the puzzle and the subject of this chapter.

Alerts generated by Falco are helpful for observing and securing your production system, and we will give you some advice on how to use those alerts proficiently. The first part of the chapter is about tools that help you consume Falco's outputs effectively. We will teach you how to get notified immediately when Falco detects a security threat, so your security team can react as soon as possible and take appropriate countermeasures. Finally, we'll show you a mechanism for automatically responding to threats to speed up response times.

Working with Falco Outputs

A minimal Falco installation outputs a simple textual log that you can store for later consultation, but this is not very useful. Fortunately, more intelligent tools allow you to work with Falco's outputs and expand its possibilities, and these are an important part of integrating Falco into your ecosystem.

This section will talk in detail about two tools that we have already mentioned in the book. The first, falco-exporter, is a tool designed to do one thing and do it well: produce metrics from Falco's detected events. The second, Falcosidekick, is the Swiss Army knife of Falco outputs. It lets you aggregate data from multiple Falco sensors, filter the notifications, and forward them to any other application or platform in your environment.

falco-exporter

The falco-exporter project (*https://oreil.ly/0j6EJ*) provides a Prometheus metrics exporter for Falco output events. It consumes Falco outputs via a streamed gRPC API and exposes a metrics endpoint. The metrics include information on the number of triggered rules and detailed information on the priority and tags associated with the rules, as well as labels to identify each event's origin, such as the hostname, namespace, and pod's name. It also provides a preconfigured Grafana dashboard.[1] falco-exporter is useful for when you only need metrics about security events. (By contrast, Falcosidekick can also export metrics, but it comes with many other functionalities and outputs.)

Before installing falco-exporter, ensure that Falco is installed and configured with the gRCP server and gRPC output enabled over a Unix socket (see "gRPC Output" on page 110 for a refresher).

Host installation

To install falco-exporter directly on the host, you have to download the latest version from the releases page (*https://oreil.ly/rfK8e*), decompress the archive, and copy the executable file *falco-exporter* to your preferred location (e.g., */usr/bin*). Whether you execute it manually or run it as a service is entirely up to you. The default options work out of the box with the gRPC Unix socket in */var/run/falco.sock* (the default option for Falco). If you need to customize its options, run `falco-exporter --help` for assistance.

Running in a container

To run falco-exporter in a container using Docker, use these commands:

```
$ docker pull falcosecurity/falco-exporter:latest
$ docker run -v /var/run/falco.sock:/var/run/falco.sock \
    falcosecurity/falco-exporter:latest
```

The `docker run` command assumes that Falco is installed on the host and Falco's gRPC Unix socket is present in */var/run/falco.sock*.

Deploying to Kubernetes

You can deploy falco-exporter to a Kubernetes cluster using either Helm or manifest files (see Chapter 9 for details on the two installation methods), but we recommend Helm. You first need to add the Falcosecurity charts repository:

---

1 A Grafana dashboard (*https://oreil.ly/2sVSm*) is a set of organized UI elements to visualize the data. Dashboard configurations can be stored in a file and shared. You can get most of the available dashboards from Grafana's online gallery (*https://oreil.ly/F25kV*).

```
$ helm repo add falcosecurity https://falcosecurity.github.io/charts
$ helm repo update
```

Then, to install the chart, run:

```
$ helm install falco-exporter falcosecurity/falco-exporter
```

For detailed instructions, see the falco-exporter chart documentation (*https://oreil.ly/ qkH5G*). If you want to use manifest files instead, follow the steps in the falco-exporter documentation (*https://oreil.ly/lktaK*).

Falcosidekick

The Falcosidekick project (*https://oreil.ly/MVyRi*) provides a complete solution for connecting Falco to your ecosystem. It works on top of Falco's output and allows you to forward its notifications to many other destinations (see Figure 12-1). Falcosidekick can add custom fields to the notifications or filter events by priority (on a per-destination basis). In particular, supported outputs include platforms and applications for:

- Communication and collaboration
- Metrics and observability
- Alerting
- Logging and storage
- Function as a Service (FaaS) and serverless
- Message queues and streaming

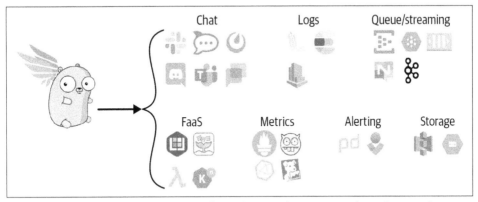

Figure 12-1. The Falcosidekick logo (left) and some of its supported notification destinations (right)

Falcosidekick also allows you to use a side project, falcosidekick-ui (*https://oreil.ly/o1pcB*), to visualize Falco events in a pleasant web UI (shown in Figure 12-2). The web UI displays statistics about detected events and shows values in aggregate form and on a timeline. You can also filter for the events you are interested in and get all the event details quickly.

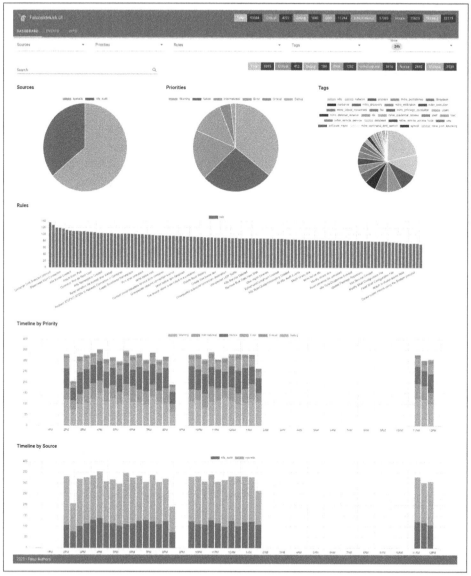

Figure 12-2. The Falcosidekick web UI

Using Falcosidekick requires a small change in Falco's configuration: before using it, enable JSON formatting and configure the HTTP output to send events to the Falcosidekick endpoint (it listens at port 2801 by default). See Chapter 8 for Falco output configuration instructions and the Falcosidekick online documentation for specific details.

Host installation

To install Falcosidekick directly on the host, download the latest version from the releases page (*https://oreil.ly/ToAMj*), decompress the archive, and copy the executable file *falcosidekick* to your preferred location (e.g., */usr/bin*). Whether to execute it manually or run it as a service is entirely up to you. You also need to create a YAML configuration file and pass its path as an argument. For example:

```
$ falcosidekick -c falcosidekick_config.yaml
```

The Falcosidekick repository includes an example configuration file that you can start with. Falcosidekick also supports environment variables that you can use as an alternative or to override the configuration file values.

Running in a container

To run Falcosidekick in a container using Docker, use these commands:

```
$ docker pull falcosecurity/falcosidekick:latest
$ docker run -d -p 2801:2801 falcosecurity/falcosidekick:latest
```

The docker run command assumes that Falco is installed on the host and that the HTTP output is configured to send events to port 2801. Using Docker's -e option, you can use environment variables to pass configurations. Alternatively, use Docker's -v option to give it a YAML configuration file.

Deploying to Kubernetes

As with falco-exporter, you can deploy Falcosidekick to a Kubernetes cluster using either Helm or manifest files. We recommend the Helm installation option, which comes in two variants. Before we explore them, if you haven't already added the Falcosecurity charts repository to Helm, do it by running:

```
$ helm repo add falcosecurity https://falcosecurity.github.io/charts
$ helm repo update
```

Now you're ready to deploy to your Kubernetes cluster. The first and more ordinary way to do this is when you already have Falco deployed and configured to send events to Falcosidekick and you just need to install the Falcosidekick chart:

```
$ helm install falcosidekick falcosecurity/falcosidekick
```

The other variant allows you to deploy Falco and Falcosidekick in a single Helm installation that will automatically configure both charts to work together. It's usually the most convenient solution. To do this, run:

```
$ helm install falco falcosecurity/falco --set falcosidekick.enabled=true
```

Optionally, if you want to deploy the Falcosidekick web UI as well, add `--set webui.enabled=true` to the install command (regardless of which variant you choose).

You can find details on additional options in the Falcosidekick chart documentation (*https://oreil.ly/QaipZ*). If you want to use manifest files instead, use the provided online examples (*https://oreil.ly/fziYL*).[2]

Observability and Analysis

Falco allows you to observe and analyze the security of your cloud-native environment. If you plan to leverage Falco's detections for auditing or forensic purposes, you'll usually want to store as much information as possible and make Falco's results easily accessible and searchable. The tools described in this chapter offer you plenty of support.

Storing Falco events is like ingesting any other application logs. This means you can reuse your existing logging backend for Falco. Also, Falcosidekick can easily send Falco events to systems that allow you to store and analyze vast volumes of log data, like Elasticsearch and Splunk. Since you will likely use this approach for later analysis, we suggest keeping all events that Falco emits with no filtering.

You'll probably also want to collect metrics, as this can help you detect errors and anomalies in your application. For instance, a metric reporting that a Falco rule regularly triggers on a particular machine may be a symptom of a security problem, a misconfiguration, or an implementation bug in your running application. A reliable tool for this purpose is falco-exporter: it exposes metrics, connects Falco to Prometheus, and also offers a ready-to-use Grafana dashboard (Figure 12-3).

---

2 The actual URLs of the Falcosidekick example manifest files for Kubernetes may change from time to time, but you can always find them under the Falcosecurity GitHub organization. Note that any Helm chart can generate such files. Indeed, like Falco's manifest files, Falcosidekick's files are rendered starting from its chart.

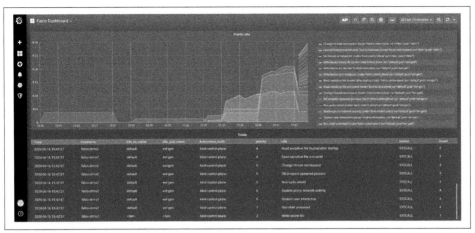

Figure 12-3. The preconfigured Grafana dashboard for Falco events metrics provided by falco-exporter

Getting Notified

Although storing and aggregating Falco events is fine for observability, it's not helpful when you need to react promptly to a security event. You likely want to receive important notifications immediately and in the right place so that you or your team can take countermeasures or start investigating right away.

Falco's built-in output channels do not provide a specific mechanism for immediate notifications, but Falcosidekick allows you to forward only important notifications. For example, let's say you want to get notifications whenever an event triggers the *Sudo Potential Privilege Escalation* rule (which comes with `priority: CRITICAL`), but not for other, noisier rules with lower priority levels. Falcosidekick allows you to configure a minimum priority level at which you want to send events to a specific destination, and to adjust this configuration for each destination. It supports most on-call systems, like PagerDuty, Opsgenie, and Prometheus Alertmanager and can send notifications to most common communication platforms, including Slack, Mattermost, Rocket.Chat, Microsoft Teams, and Discord.

You can use Falcosidekick configurations to integrate Falco alerts into your existing environment easily. And because Falcosidekick allows you to forward Falco notifications to multiple destinations simultaneously, you can, for example, send the alerts to both PagerDuty and a Slack channel.

Responding to Threats

Another meaningful—and more sophisticated—way of consuming Falco events is to create systems that automatically take action in response to threats or security incidents. Implementing custom actions in response to threats is easier than you might think.

Although The Falco Project does not provide a specific tool for this purpose, a few emerging projects in the community are implementing this concept. Such systems are sometimes called *response engines* and usually specialize in managing threats in Kubernetes.

A response engine provides a straightforward mechanism to perform a predefined task when a Falco rule condition is violated. You can create a simple implementation using Falcosidekick to forward Falco notifications to a FaaS platform or serverless solution that, in turn, performs the required action. For example, you can automatically terminate a Kubernetes Pod whenever a Falco rule determines that the Pod is compromised, by implementing a cloud function that uses the Kubernetes API to delete the compromised Pod. Figure 12-4 illustrates this approach and shows some cloud function providers supported by Falcosidekick.

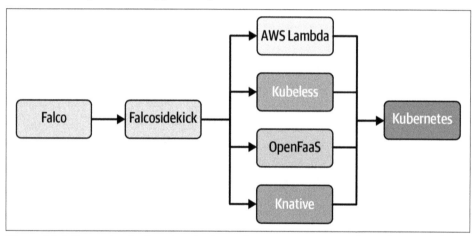

Figure 12-4. Example of a functional scheme for a response engine for Kubernetes that uses Falcosidekick outputs to perform actions

You might want to be notified regardless of the rule's priority level, but you will probably only want to perform actions for specific rules. For example, you might want only rules with a CRITICAL priority level to terminate Pods. Falcosidekick helps with this because it allows you to filter notifications based on their priority value, so you can control the information each destination receives.

We advise you to analyze your needs and design your response engine to meet them. Falco and tools like Falcosidekick will provide everything you need to support your solution.

Conclusion

This chapter concludes Part III. You've learned all the fundamental aspects of running Falco in production and can now configure and customize it for almost any need and scenario. You've also discovered how to consume Falco events properly and integrate them with your ecosystem.

In Part IV, you will go beyond the knowledge of the average user and learn how to extend Falco to satisfy any advanced requirement.

PART IV

Extending Falco

CHAPTER 13

Writing Falco Rules

Welcome to Part IV of the book! Now that you've learned what Falco is and does (Part I), understand the intricacies of its architecture (Part II), and are a pro at deploying and running it (Part III), it's time, once more, to step up your game.

The final part of this book (Chapters 13 through 15) is about going beyond what comes out of the box. You will learn how to customize Falco for your specific needs and how, if you desire, you can contribute your improvements to the project so that the community can benefit from them. This is where you get to unleash your creativity.

We've already covered rules extensively in the book, in particular in Chapter 7. But you unlock the true power of Falco when you become capable of creating your own rules and adapting the existing ones to your environment—which is what we're going to show you how to do here.

This chapter assumes you have a good understanding of fields and filters (covered in Chapter 6) and of the basics of rules and rules files (Chapter 7). If you feel you need a refresher, just go back to those chapters. We'll wait for you here until you're ready.

Customizing the Default Falco Rules

Although Falco's default set of rules is rich and constantly expanding, it's not uncommon to encounter situations where those rules require customization. Here are some examples:

- You want to expand the scope of a rule or increase its coverage.
- You want to tighten the number of rules that Falco loads to decrease its CPU usage.

- You want to reduce alerting noise by controlling a rule's behavior or adding exceptions to it.

Falco offers a framework to accomplish these things without having to fork the default rules files and maintain your own copies. Chapter 7 taught you how to replace and append to macros, lists, and rules, as well as how to disable rules. This is especially useful since, as you learned in Chapter 10, the order in which rules files are loaded is important, and you control that order. This means you can change an existing rule in a separate file that is loaded later in the initialization chain.

The default Falco configuration is crafted to take advantage of this mechanism, providing two places out of the box where you can customize existing rules without touching the default ruleset. The first is *falco_rules.local.yaml*. This file, which is initially empty, is loaded after *falco_rules.yaml* and is therefore a good place to disable or modify rules in the default ruleset. The second is */etc/falco/rules.d*. Falco, by default, loads all the rules files that it finds in this directory after loading *falco_rules.yaml* and *falco_rules.local.yaml*. This makes it another good place for customizations.

Writing New Falco Rules

At its core, writing a new rule is just a matter of crafting the condition and the output, so conceptually it is a very straightforward process. In practice, however, there are several factors to take into account. Improvised rule development often results in imperfect or even nonfunctional rules. Seasoned Falco users tend to develop their own processes for rule writing, and we recommend you do the same. What the best process is depends on your setup, target environment, and taste, so we won't be able to offer you absolute prescriptions. Instead, we'll share the way we do it, hoping it can serve as inspiration and guidance.

Our Rule Development Method

The method for rule development used by this book's authors consists of nine steps:

1. Replicate the events you want to detect.
2. Capture the events and save them in a trace file.
3. Craft and test the condition filter with the aid of sysdig.
4. Craft and test the output with the aid of sysdig.
5. Convert the sysdig command line into a rule.
6. Validate the rule in Falco.
7. Modularize and optimize the rule.

8. Create a regression.

9. Share the rule with the community.

In the following sections we'll expand on each item in this list and provide a real-world example, walking you through crafting a new rule that detects attempts to create symlinks[1] inside the */proc*, */bin*, and */etc* directories. This is, at minimum, strange behavior and could potentially indicate fishy activity. Here's how you would apply our method to build such a rule.

1. Replicate the events you want to detect

It's almost impossible to create a reliable rule without testing and validating it, so the first step is to re-create the scenario (or scenarios) that the rule should detect. In this case, you want to detect the creation of symlinks in three specific directories. You can re-create that scenario from within a terminal using the ln command:

```
$ ln -s ~ /proc/evillink
$ ln -s ~ /bin/evillink
$ ln -s ~ /etc/evillink
```

2. Capture the events and save them in a trace file

Now you can capture the suspicious activity using sysdig. (If you need a refresher on sysdig and trace files, go back to "Observing System Calls" on page 43.) sysdig allows you to easily store the activity in a trace file using the -w command-line flag. To see how it works, issue this command in a terminal:

```
$ sysdig -w evillinks.scap
```

In another terminal, run the three ln commands again, then go back to the first terminal and stop sysdig with Ctrl-C. You now have your activity in a trace file that you can inspect as many times you want:

```
$ sysdig -r evillinks.scap
```

You will notice that the trace file contains all of the host's activity, not only your ln commands. You will also notice that the file is pretty big. You can make it smaller and easier to inspect by using a filter when you run the capture:

```
$ sysdig -w evillinks.scap proc.name=ln
```

Now you have a noise-free file that is less than 1 MB in size, containing only the specific activity that you need to craft your rule. Saving the rule-triggering activity in a trace file has several advantages:

---

1 The term *symlink* is short for *symbolic link*; in Unix, it indicates a filesystem entry that is a reference to another file or directory.

- It requires replicating complex behaviors only once. (Not all suspicious behaviors are as simple to detect as running ln three times!)

- It allows you to focus on the events and stay in a single terminal, without having to replicate the rule-triggering commands many times.

- It allows you to develop rules on a different machine. You don't even need to deploy and configure Falco on the machine where the behavior is happening! This is really nice if you want to capture behaviors in "unfriendly" environments like cloud containers or edge devices.

- It lets you develop rules with normal user privileges.

- It provides consistency, which is useful not only for creating the rule but also for implementing regressions when the rule is done.

3. Craft and test the condition filter with the aid of sysdig

Now that you have the data you need, it's time to work on the condition. Typically, at this stage you'll want to answer a couple of questions:

1. What type of system call (or system calls) do you need to target? Of course, not all Falco rules are based on system calls; for example, you might be using a plugin. But in general, identifying the type of event that will trigger the rule is the first order of business.

2. Once you know which event to parse, which of its parameters or arguments do you need to check?

sysdig can help you answer these questions. Use it to read and decode the capture file:

```
$ sysdig -r evillinks.scap
```

Toward the end of the output file is where the magic happens:

```
2313 11:21:22.782601383 1 ln (23859) > symlinkat
2314 11:21:22.782662611 1 ln (23859) < symlinkat res=0 target=/home/foo
linkdirfd=-100(AT_FDCWD) linkpath=/etc/evillink
```

Our system call is symlinkat. The system call's manpage (*https://oreil.ly/oW7rT*) tells you that it's a variation of another system call, symlink. You can also see that the linkpath argument contains the filesystem path of the symbolic link. This is exactly what you need to know to craft your filter, which should look like this:

```
(evt.type=symlink or evt.type=symlinkat) and (
  evt.arg.linkpath startswith /proc/ or
  evt.arg.linkpath startswith /bin/ or
  evt.arg.linkpath startswith /etc/
)
```

You can immediately leverage sysdig to validate that this is the right filter:

```
$ sysdig -r evillinks.scap \
  "(evt.type=symlink or evt.type=symlinkat) and \
  (evt.arg.linkpath startswith /proc/ or \
  evt.arg.linkpath startswith /bin/ or \
  evt.arg.linkpath startswith /etc/)"
438 11:21:13.204948767 2 ln (23814) < symlinkat res=-2(ENOENT) target=/home/foo
linkdirfd=-100(AT_FDCWD) linkpath=/proc/evillink
1679 11:21:19.420360948 0 ln (23850) < symlinkat res=0 target=/home/foo
linkdirfd=-100(AT_FDCWD) linkpath=/bin/evillink
2314 11:21:22.782662611 1 ln (23859) < symlinkat res=0 target=/home/foo
linkdirfd=-100(AT_FDCWD) linkpath=/etc/evillink
```

Bingo! The output correctly shows the three system calls that should trigger the rule.

4. Craft and test the output with the aid of sysdig

sysdig, handily, can help you craft the rule's output too. The sysdig -p flag, in particular, receives a Falco output–compatible string as input and uses it to print a Falco-like output to the terminal for each event accepted by the filter. This makes it effortless to craft and test the rule's output, knowing that Falco will show the same thing when the rule triggers. For example, this looks like a nice output for your rule:

```
a symlink was created in a sensitive directory (link=%evt.arg.linkpath,
target=%evt.arg.target, cmd=%proc.cmdline)
```

Test it, together with the filter, in sysdig:

```
$ sysdig -r evillinks.scap \
  -p"a symlink was created in a sensitive directory \
  (link=%evt.arg.linkpath, target=%evt.arg.target, cmd=%proc.cmdline)" \
  "(evt.type=symlink or evt.type=symlinkat) and \
  (evt.arg.linkpath startswith /proc/ or \
  evt.arg.linkpath startswith /bin/ or \
  evt.arg.linkpath startswith /etc/)"
a symlink was created in a sensitive directory (link=/proc/evillink,
target=/home/foo, cmd=ln -s /home/foo /proc/evillink)
a symlink was created in a sensitive directory (link=/bin/evillink,
target=/home/foo, cmd=ln -s /home/foo /bin/evillink)
a symlink was created in a sensitive directory (link=/etc/evillink,
target=/home/foo, cmd=ln -s /home/foo /etc/evillink)
```

Note the quotation marks around both the filter and the output condition. This prevents the shell from getting confused by any characters they contain.

Your condition and output look pretty good. Time to switch to Falco!

5. Convert the sysdig command line into a rule

The next step is converting what you have into a Falco rule. This is little more than a copy-and-paste exercise, since you already know that the condition and output work:

```
- rule: Symlink in a Sensitive Directory
  desc: >
```

```
        Detect the creation of a symbolic link
        in a sensitive directory like /etc or /bin.
      condition: >
        (evt.type=symlink or evt.type=symlinkat) and (
          evt.arg.linkpath startswith /proc/ or
          evt.arg.linkpath startswith /bin/ or
          evt.arg.linkpath startswith /etc/)
      output: >
        a symlink was created in a sensitive directory
        (link=%evt.arg.linkpath, target=%evt.arg.target, cmd=%proc.cmdline)
      priority: WARNING
```

6. Validate the rule in Falco

Save the rule in a YAML file called *symlink.yaml*. Now testing it in Falco is a matter of
loading it with the -r flag, then using the -e flag to use the capture file as input:

```
$ falco -r symlink.yaml -e evillinks.scap
2022-02-05T01:09:23+0000: Falco version 0.31.0 (driver version
319368f1ad778691164d33d59945e00c5752cd27)
2022-02-05T01:09:23+0000: Falco initialized with configuration file
/etc/falco/falco.yaml
2022-02-05T01:09:23+0000: Loading rules from file symlink.yaml:
2022-02-05T01:09:23+0000: Reading system call events from file: evillinks.scap
2022-02-04T19:21:13.204948767+0000: Warning a symlink was created in a
sensitive directory (link=/proc/evillink, target=/home/foo, cmd=ln -s /home/foo
/proc/evillink)
2022-02-04T19:21:19.420360948+0000: Warning a symlink was created in a
sensitive directory (link=/bin/evillink, target=/home/foo, cmd=ln -s /home/foo
/bin/evillink)
2022-02-04T19:21:22.782662611+0000: Warning a symlink was created in a
sensitive directory (link=/etc/evillink, target=/home/foo, cmd=ln -s /home/foo
/etc/evillink)
Events detected: 3
Rule counts by severity:
   WARNING: 3
Triggered rules by rule name:
   Symlink in a Sensitive Directory: 3
Syscall event drop monitoring:
   - event drop detected: 0 occurrences
   - num times actions taken: 0
```

The rule triggered the expected number of times and displayed the correct output.
Congratulations!

Note how, in Falco, you can leverage the same trace file that you created with sysdig.
The -e command-line option tells Falco: "Read system calls from the given file
instead of using a driver. When you reach the end of the file, print a summary and
return." Very handy for quick iteration!

---

7. Modularize and optimize the rule

You have a working rule and you've tested it, but there's room to make it prettier. Step 7 is adding modularity to the rule:

```
- macro: sensitive_sylink_dir
  condition: >
    (evt.arg.linkpath startswith /proc/ or
     evt.arg.linkpath startswith /bin/ or
     evt.arg.linkpath startswith /etc/)

- macro: create_symlink
  condition: (evt.type=symlink or evt.type=symlinkat)

- rule: Symlink in a Sensitive Directory
  desc: >
    Detect the creation of a symbolic link
    in a sensitive directory like /etc or /bin.
  condition:  create_symlink and sensitive_sylink_dir
  output: >
    a symlink was created in a sensitive directory
    (link=%evt.arg.linkpath, target=%evt.arg.target, cmd=%proc.cmdline)
  priority: WARNING
```

This moves the condition's checks into macros, which makes the condition shorter and more readable. That's great, but you can do even better:

```
- list: symlink_syscalls
  items: [symlink, symlinkat]
- list: sensitive_dirs
  items: [/proc/, /bin/, /etc/]

- macro: create_symlink
  condition: (evt.type in (symlink_syscalls))
- macro: sensitive_sylink_dir
  condition: (evt.arg.linkpath pmatch (sensitive_dirs))

- rule: Symlink in a Sensitive Directory
  desc: >
    Detect the creation of a symbolic link
    in a sensitive directory like /etc or /bin.
  condition:  create_symlink and sensitive_sylink_dir
  output: >
    a symlink was created in a sensitive directory
    (link=%evt.arg.linkpath, target=%evt.arg.target, cmd=%proc.cmdline)
  priority: WARNING
```

What you did here is to move the condition constants into lists. This has multiple benefits. First, it makes the rule easy to extend, in a noninvasive way. If you want to add another sensitive directory, you can do it easily by adding the relevant item to the list or, even better, by creating a second symlink_syscalls list in append mode.

This also gives you an opportunity to optimize the rule by using operators like in and pmatch that can perform multiple checks in an efficient way.

8. Create a regression

When you create a new rule, particularly if your goal is including it in the official ruleset, you might like to be able to test it in the future. For example, you might want to ensure it still works with new versions of Falco or on different Linux distributions. You might also want to measure its performance (such as its CPU utilization) under stress. The capture file you created at the beginning of the process is a good base for a regression.

As an alternative, the Falco community has created a tool called event-generator (mentioned in Chapter 2) that's useful for testing. If you add an action for your rule in event-generator, you or other people will be able to trigger the rule in real time on an arbitrary machine. The tool can replay your rule-triggering scenario in a flexible way, including triggering the rule multiple times and at specific frequencies. That way, you can precisely measure its CPU utilization. You can also check if, under heavy stress, the rule will slow Falco down to the point where the driver starts dropping system calls.

A full discussion of event-generator goes beyond the scope of this book, but you can take a look at its GitHub repository (*https://oreil.ly/jERpD*) to learn more about it.

9. Share the rule with the community

Congratulations, you've completed the development of a brand new rule! At this point, it is important to remember that Falco is a tool written by the community for the community. Every new rule you write could be valuable to many others, so you should consider contributing it to the default ruleset. Chapter 15 will teach you everything you need to know about contributing to Falco. As Falco maintainers and community members, we'd like to thank you in advance for any rules you decide to share with the community.

Things to Keep in Mind When Writing Rules

Now that we've covered the basics, let's discuss some concepts that are a bit more advanced but very important to keep in mind when developing rules.

Priorities

As mentioned in Chapter 7, every Falco rule must have a priority. The rule priority is typically reported in conjunction with the output and can have one of the following values:

- EMERGENCY

- ALERT

- CRITICAL

- ERROR

- WARNING

- NOTICE

- INFORMATIONAL

- DEBUG

Picking the right priorities for your rules is crucial, because typically rules are filtered based on priority. Assigning too high a priority to a rule could cause alert flooding and diminish its value.

Here is what the official Falco documentation has to say about how priorities are used in the default ruleset:

- If a rule is related to writing state (filesystem, etc.), its priority is ERROR.
- If a rule is related to an unauthorized read of state (reading sensitive files, etc.), its priority is WARNING.
- If a rule is related to unexpected behavior (spawning an unexpected shell in a container, opening an unexpected network connection, etc.), its priority is NOTICE.
- If a rule is related to behaving against good practices (unexpected privileged containers, containers with sensitive mounts, running interactive commands as root), its priority is INFORMATIONAL.

Noise

Noise is one of the most critical factors to take into account when crafting rules, as well as a generally complex topic in security. The trade-off between detection accuracy and false positive generation is a constant source of tension in detection tools like Falco.

It's often said that the only ruleset with no false positives is one with no rules. Completely avoiding false positives is extremely difficult and often an unrealistic goal, but there are some guidelines you can follow to reduce the problem:

Guideline 1: Test and validate.
Before using a rule in production, make sure you test it extensively in as many environments as possible (different OS distributions, kernels, container engines, and orchestrators).

Guideline 2: Priorities, and priority-based filtering, are your friends.

Avoid deploying a rule for the first time with ERROR or CRITICAL as the priority. Start with DEBUG or INFO, see what happens, and increase the value if it's not too noisy. Lower-priority rules can be easily filtered out at different stages of the output pipeline, so they don't run the risk of waking up the security operations center team in the middle of the night.

Guideline 3: Leverage tags.

The tags that you assign to your rules are included in Falco's gRPC and JSON outputs. This means you can use them to complement priorities and filter Falco's output in an even more flexible way.

Guideline 4: Plan for exceptions.

Good rules are designed to account for known and unknown exceptions in a way that is readable and modular and can easily be extended.

Take a look, for example, at the *Write below rpm database* rule from the default ruleset:

```
- rule: Write below rpm database
  desc: an attempt to write to the rpm database by any non-rpm related program
  condition: >
    fd.name startswith /var/lib/rpm and open_write
    and not rpm_procs
    and not ansible_running_python
    and not python_running_chef
    and not exe_running_docker_save
    and not amazon_linux_running_python_yum
    and not user_known_write_rpm_database_activities
  output: >
    Rpm database opened for writing by a non-rpm program
    (command=%proc.cmdline file=%fd.name
    parent=%proc.pname pcmdline=%proc.pcmdline
    container_id=%container.id image=%container.image.repository)
  priority: ERROR
  tags: [filesystem, software_mgmt, mitre_persistence]
```

Note how known exceptions are included in the rule as macros (rpm_procs, ansible_running_python, etc.), but the rule also includes a macro (user_known_write_rpm_database_activities) that lets the user add their own exceptions through the override mechanism.

Performance

Performance is another important topic to consider when writing and deploying rules, because Falco typically operates with high-frequency data sources. When you are using Falco with a system call source like the kernel module or the eBPF probe, your whole ruleset might need to be evaluated millions of times per second. At such frequencies, rule performance is key.

Having a tight ruleset is definitely a good practice to keep Falco's CPU utilization under control, as you learned in Chapter 10. It is also important, however, to make sure every new rule you create is optimized for performance. The overhead of your rule is more or less proportional to the number of field comparisons that the rule's condition needs to perform for every input event. Therefore, you should expect that a simple condition like this:

```
proc.name=p1
```

will use around 20% of the CPU of a more complex rule like this one:

```
proc.name=p1 or proc.name=p2 or proc.name=p3 or proc.name=p4 or proc.name=p5
```

Optimizing a rule is all about making sure that, in most common situations, it requires the Falco engine to perform the smallest possible number of comparisons.

Here are some guidelines you should follow to reduce the CPU utilization of your rules:

- The rule should always start with a check on the event type (such as evt.type=open or evt.type in (mkdir, mkdirat)). Falco is smart about this: it understands when your rule is restricted to only some event types and will evaluate the rule only when it receives a matching event. In other words, if your rule starts with evt.type=open, Falco won't even start evaluating it for any event that is not an open system call. This is so effective (and important!) that Falco emits a warning when a rule doesn't include a check on the event type.

- Include aggressive comparisons that have a high probability of failing earlier, rather than later, in your rule. A Falco condition works like an if statement in a programming language: it's evaluated left to right until something fails. The sooner you make the condition fail, the less work it will require to complete. Try to find simple ways to restrict the scope of your rule. Can you limit it to specific processes, files, or containers? Can you apply it to only a subset of users? Encode these restrictions in the rule, toward the beginning.

- Heavy, complex rule logic should be included after (to the right of) the aggressive comparisons and restrictions. For example, long exception lists belong at the end of the rule.

- Whenever possible, use multiple value operators like in and pmatch instead of writing multiple comparisons. In other words, evt.type in (mkdir, mkdirat) is better than evt.type=mkdir or evt.type=mkdirat. Multiple value operators are heavily optimized and become progressively more effective as the number of values grows.

- In general, small is good. Develop the habit of keeping things as simple as possible. This will not only speed up processing of your rules, it will also ensure they are readable and maintainable!

Tagging

Tagging is a powerful tool for crafting rules. It has three important uses: flexibly filtering the rules Falco loads, adding context to its output, and supporting notification filtering and prioritization, therefore reducing noise. Using tags generously will improve your Falco experience and ensure you get the most out of your rules.

Conclusion

This was an intense chapter! Rule writing is a demanding topic, but it can also be fun and creative. Plus, writing the perfect rule to perform an impressive detection will earn you a lot of points with your coworkers.

CHAPTER 14

Falco Development

Extending Falco is the best way to ensure that it perfectly fits your unique requirements. This chapter will show you three approaches to Falco development. We'll begin with an overview of Falco's codebase and a quick guide to building Falco from the source, which allows you to work with Falco's code directly. This first approach gives you more freedom but is more difficult and perhaps less convenient than the other two. The second approach lets you build an application that processes Falco notifications in the desired way by interfacing with the gRPC API. The third is the standard and easiest way of extending Falco: writing your own plugin.

For the last two approaches, we will teach you by using examples. We use the Go programming language in these code snippets, so some familiarity with it will be helpful, but it's not strictly required. This chapter also assumes that you have read Part II of this book. If you are concerned that this material may be too difficult, don't be scared: we think you'll find it understandable and interesting even if you are not a developer.

Programming Languages for Falco Development

Falco's core is written mainly in C++, with some low-level components in C (like *libscap* and the drivers). To fully understand the codebase or work with the core components, a good knowledge of C/C++ is required. However, Falco also exposes the gRPC and Plugin APIs, which you can use to develop components for Falco in virtually any programming language you like. Using these APIs is our preferred way of extending Falco and does not require you to stick with C/C++.

Go is the most common language for interfacing with Falco's APIs, because it's been so widely adopted in cloud native software. You will notice that most Falcosecurity libraries, SDKs, and tools use Go. For the same reason, we use Go in the code snippets included in this chapter, and you'll need to install Go if you want to run them.

> If you want to use another programming language, the general concepts described in this chapter still apply, so we recommend reading on.

Working with the Codebase

Falco is open source, and all its source code lives in GitHub under the Falcosecuriy organization. All you need to start navigating the codebase is a browser. If you want to store the source code locally and open it with your preferred editor, you will need to use Git.

The Falcosecurity organization hosts Falco and many other related projects. The community is very active, so you will also find many experimental projects. The core of The Falco Project lives in two main repositories: *falcosecurity/falco* and *falcosecurity/libs*.

The falcosecurity/falco Repository

The *falcosecurity/falco* repository (*https://oreil.ly/lqnL4*) contains the source code of the *falco* user-space program (the one you usually interact with). It's the main and most important repository. The project is organized as follows:

/cmake
> Here you can find cmake modules that the Falco build system uses to pull dependencies and implement specific functionalities, including cmake files to pull the *falcosecurity/libs* source code during the build process.

/docker
> This folder is organized into various subdirectories, each containing the source code of a Falco container image. Some are not published because they are for development use only. See the README file (*https://oreil.ly/oiGQQ*) for details.

/proposals
> This folder includes design proposals made by the community and approved by maintainers. You may find useful information here that helps you understand how the Falco authors made certain architectural decisions and the rationale behind them.

/rules
> The default rules files live here.

/scripts
> Various script files live inside this folder. For example, this is where you'll find the *falco-driver-loader* script's source code.

/test and /tests

These two folders contain regression tests and unit tests for Falco, respectively.

/userspace

The actual C++ source code of Falco lives inside this folder. Its contents are organized into two subdirectories: *engine*, which contains the rule engine implementation, and *falco*, which contains the implementations of high-level features like the output channels, the gRPC server, and the CLI application.

Although this is the main Falco repository, not all of the project's source code lives here. Most is actually in the *falcosecurity/libs* repository, which contains the implementations of Falco's core low-level logic.

The falcosecurity/libs Repository

Throughout this book, we have mentioned *libscap*, *libsinsp*, and the drivers many times. The *falcosecurity/libs* repository (*https://oreil.ly/HSLDT*) hosts the source code of those components. It is organized as follows:

/cmake/modules

This folder contains cmake modules to pull external dependencies and module definitions for *libscap* and *libsinsp* that consumer applications (like Falco) can use.

/driver

This folder includes the source code for the kernel module and eBPF probe (mainly in C).

/proposals

Similar to the one in the Falco repository, this folder contains the design proposal documents.

/userspace

Organized into several subdirectories, here you can find the source code (in C and C++) of *libsinsp* and *libscap* along with other shared code.

This repository contains all the low-level logic required for kernel instrumentation and data enrichment. The filtering grammar, plugin framework implementation, and many other functionalities are hosted here. The *libs* codebase is vast, but don't let that frighten you: all you need to understand it is a good knowledge of C/C++.

Building Falco from Source

Compiling Falco from its source is similar to compiling any other C++ project that uses cmake. The build system requires a handful of dependencies: cmake, make, gcc, wget, and of course git. (You also need Git to get a local copy of the Falco repository.)

You can find instructions on how to install those dependencies in the documentation (*https://oreil.ly/UMJI2*).

Once you have ensured that the required dependencies are installed on your system, use the following command to get a local copy of the repository:

```
$ git clone git@github.com:falcosecurity/falco.git
```

Git will clone the repository into a newly created folder called *falco*. Enter that directory:

```
$ cd falco
```

Prepare a directory to contain the build files, then enter it:

```
$ mkdir -p build
$ cd build
```

Finally, inside the build directory, run:

```
$ cmake -DUSE_BUNDLED_DEPS=On ..
$ make falco
```

This command will likely take a substantial amount of time the first time you run it, as cmake downloads and builds all the dependencies. This is because we configured it with -DUSE_BUNDLED_DEPS=On; alternatively, you can set -DUSE_BUNDLED_DEPS=Off to use system dependencies, but if you do this, you will need to manually install all the required dependencies on your system before building Falco. You can find an updated list of dependencies and other useful cmake options in the documentation.

After the make command completes, if there were no errors, you should find the newly created Falco executable in *./userspace/falco/falco* (the path is relative to the build directory).

Now, if you also want to build the driver from the source and you already have the kernel headers installed in your system, run:

```
$ make driver
```

This command only builds the kernel module, by default. If you want to build the eBPF probe instead, use:

```
$ cmake -DBUILD_BPF=True ..
$ make bpf
```

In both cases, you will find the newly built driver under *./driver* (the path is relative to the build directory).

Extending Falco Using the gRPC API

Although you might be tempted to introduce a new feature directly into the codebase, there are more convenient ways. For example, if you want to extend Falco's output mechanism, you can create a program that works on top of Falco and implements your business logic. In particular, the gRPC API allows your program to consume Falco notifications and receive metadata easily.

This section will use an example program to show you how to start developing with the Falco gRPC API. To follow along, you'll need a running Falco instance with the gRCP server and gRPC output channel enabled (see Chapter 8). You will use gRPC via a Unix socket, so make sure you have installed and configured Falco accordingly.

We use the *client-go* library (*https://oreil.ly/1bSay*) in the following example, which makes using the gRPC API straightforward:

```
package main

import (
    "context"
    "fmt"
    "time"

    "github.com/falcosecurity/client-go/pkg/api/outputs" ❶
    "github.com/falcosecurity/client-go/pkg/client" ❶
)

func main() {

    // Set up a connection to Falco via a Unix socket
    c, err := client.NewForConfig(context.Background(), &client.Config{
        UnixSocketPath: "unix:///var/run/falco.sock", ❷
    })
    if err != nil {
        panic(err)
    }
    defer c.Close()

    // Subscribe to a stream of Falco notifications
    err = c.OutputsWatch(context.Background(), ❸
        func(res *outputs.Response) error {
            // Put your business logic here
            fmt.Println(res.Output, res.OutputFields) ❹
            return nil
        }, time.Second)
    if err != nil {
        panic(err)
    }
}
```

❶ We start by importing the *client-go* library (*https://oreil.ly/iQD2m*).

❷ The main function sets up a connection (represented by the variable c) to Falco's gRPC server via the Unix socket using the default path.

❸ The connection c allows it to call the OutputsWatch function, which subscribes to a stream of notifications and processes any incoming notification using a callback function.

❹ This example uses an anonymous function (*https://oreil.ly/f4htn*) that prints the notification to standard output. In a real-world application, you would implement your own business logic to consume Falco notifications.

Using the gRPC API to implement programs that interact with Falco is convenient and straightforward. If, instead, you need to make Falco work with other data sources, the plugin system is likely what you are looking for.

Extending Falco with Plugins

Plugins are the main way to extend Falco, and we've mentioned them many times throughout the book. To recap briefly, plugins are shared libraries (*https://oreil.ly/ EkUs3*) that conform to specific APIs. In the Falco plugin framework, the primary responsibilities of plugins are adding new data sources by connecting Falco to external sources and producing events, and extracting data from events by exporting lists of fields and decoding event data to produce field values when Falco requires them.

Plugins contain the logic to produce and interpret data. This is powerful because it means that Falco is only concerned with gathering field values from plugins and composing them into rule conditions. In other words, Falco only knows which fields can be used and how to get their values; everything else is delegated to the plugins. Thanks to this system, you can connect Falco to any domain.

There are a few important aspects to consider when designing a plugin. First, a plugin with event sourcing capability implicitly defines the event payload format (the serialized raw event data that the plugin returns to the framework). The same plugin, or other plugins with field extraction capability compatible with that data source, will be able to access the payload later, when extracting fields. Second, a plugin with field extraction capability explicitly defines fields that are bound to a data source. Finally, rules rely on data source specifications to consume the events in the format they expect.

Since describing every single technical aspect of plugin development would require a dedicated book, in this section we'll just offer an educational example of how to implement a plugin that can both generate events and extract fields. For more extensive coverage, refer to the documentation (*https://oreil.ly/004ur*).

Our example will implement a plugin that reads from the bash history file (by default located at *~/.bash_history*). Each time a user enters a command in the shell, bash stores that command line. When the shell session ends, bash appends the entered command lines in the history file. It's basically a log file. Although it has no compelling use cases, it's a simple way to learn how to create a plugin that generates events from a log file. So, let's start having fun with a bit of Go code.

Preparing a Plugin in Go

First, create a file (we called ours *myplugin.go*) and import a bunch of Go packages to simplify development. You'll also import *tail* (*https://oreil.ly/BdIXO*), a library that emulates the `tail` command (*https://oreil.ly/OWco5*) (our example uses it to read from the log file), and a set of packages from Falcosecurity's Plugin SDK for Go (*https://oreil.ly/lnyhl*) that let you implement a source plugin with that extractor capability. You must use the `main` package, or Go won't allow you to compile it as a shared object:

```go
package main

import (
    "encoding/json"
    "fmt"
    "io"
    "os"
    "time"

    "github.com/hpcloud/tail"

    "github.com/falcosecurity/plugin-sdk-go/pkg/sdk"
    "github.com/falcosecurity/plugin-sdk-go/pkg/sdk/plugins"
    "github.com/falcosecurity/plugin-sdk-go/pkg/sdk/plugins/extractor"
    "github.com/falcosecurity/plugin-sdk-go/pkg/sdk/plugins/source"
)
```

The SDK defines a set of interfaces that help you implement a plugin by following a simplified, well-defined pattern. As you will see in a moment, you have to satisfy those interfaces by adding methods—also called functions with receivers (*https://oreil.ly/t5aAZ*) in Go—to a couple of data structures that represent your plugin. Under the hood, the SDK exports those methods as the calling convention functions (or simply C symbols) required by the plugin framework. (See "Falco Plugins" on page 58 if you need a refresher on this.)

Plugin State and Initialization

The SDK requires a data structure that represents the plugin and its state. It can implement various composable interfaces, but all types of plugins must implement, at minimum, `Info` to expose general information about the plugin and `Init` to initialize the plugin with a given configuration string.

The example calls this data structure `bashPlugin`. You'll also define another data structure (called `bashPluginCfg`) that represents the plugin's configuration, to store options inside it. This isn't mandatory, but it's usually convenient:

```
// bashPluginCfg represents the plugin configuration.
type bashPluginCfg struct {
    Path string
}

// bashPlugin holds the state of the plugin.
type bashPlugin struct {
    plugins.BasePlugin
    config bashPluginCfg
}
```

Now you'll implement the first required method that exposes general information about the plugin:

```
func (b *bashPlugin) Info() *plugins.Info {
    return &plugins.Info{
        ID:          999,
        Name:        "bash",
        Description: "A Plugin that reads from ~/.bash_history",
        Version:     "0.1.0",
        EventSource: "bash",
    }
}
```

The ID field is required for all source plugins and must be unique across them to ensure interoperability. The special value 999 is reserved for development purposes only; if you intend to distribute your plugin, you should register it in the plugins registry (https://oreil.ly/7C9n1) to get a unique ID.

Another important field for interoperability is `EventSource`, where you can declare the name of the data source. Extractor plugins can use that value to determine whether they are compatible with the data source.

The other required method is `Init`. Falco calls this method only once, when loading the plugin, and passes the configuration string (the one defined in the Falco configuration for the plugin). Commonly, the configuration string is JSON-formatted. Our example first sets a default value for a member of `b.config` (an instance of the data structure for the plugin configuration that we declared earlier). Then, if the given `config` string is not empty, the function decodes the JSON value into `b.config`:

```
func (b *bashPlugin) Init(config string) error {

    // default value
    homeDir, _ := os.UserHomeDir()
```

```
    b.config.Path = homeDir + "/.bash_history"

    // skip empty config
    if config == "" {
        return nil
    }

    // else parse the provided config
    return json.Unmarshal([]byte(config), &b.config)
}
```

Adding Event Sourcing Capability

Specifically for plugins with event sourcing capability, the SDK requires another data structure that represents a *capture session* (a stream of events). It also requires the following methods:

- Open to start and initialize a capture session
- NextBatch to produce events

Falco calls Open immediately after initialization. That represents the beginning of a capture session. The method's main responsibility is instantiating the data structure that holds the session state (bashInstance in our example). Specifically, here we make a *tail.Tail instance (that mimics the behavior of tail -f -n 0) and store it in t. Then we create a bashInstance instance (to which we can assign t) and return it:

```
// bashInstance holds the state of the current session.
type bashInstance struct {
    source.BaseInstance
    t      *tail.Tail
    ticker *time.Ticker
}

func (b *bashPlugin) Open(params string) (source.Instance, error) {
    t, err := tail.TailFile(b.config.Path, tail.Config{
        Follow: true,
        Location: &tail.SeekInfo{
            Offset: 0,
            Whence: os.SEEK_END,
        },
    })
    if err != nil {
        return nil, err
    }

    return &bashInstance{
        t:      t,
        ticker: time.NewTicker(time.Millisecond * 30),
```

```
        }, nil
    }
```

The plugin system stores the value returned by Open and passes it as an argument
to the most important method for a source plugin: NextBatch. Unlike the other
methods, this belongs to the session data structure (bashInstance) and not to the
plugin data structure (bashPlugin). During the capture session, Falco repeatedly calls
NextBatch, which in turn produces a batch of new events. A batch's maximum size
depends on the size of its underlying reusable memory buffer. However, a batch can
have fewer events than its maximum capacity; it can contain just one event or even
be empty. This method usually implements the core business logic of a source plugin,
but this example just implements some simple logic: it tries to receive lines from the
b.t.Lines channel and add them to the batch. If there are none, it will time out after
a while:

```
func (b *bashInstance) NextBatch(
        bp sdk.PluginState,
        evts sdk.EventWriters,
) (int, error) {
    i := 0
    b.ticker.Reset(time.Millisecond * 30)

    for i < evts.Len() {
        select {
        case line := <-b.t.Lines:
            if line.Err != nil {
                return i, line.Err
            }

            // Add an event to the batch
            evt := evts.Get(i)
            if _, err := evt.Writer().Write([]byte(line.Text)); err != nil {
                return i, err
            }
            i++
        case <-b.ticker.C:
            // Timeout occurred, return early
            return i, sdk.ErrTimeout
        }
    }

    // The batch is full
    return i, nil
}
```

As you can see, the SDK provides an sdk.EventWriters interface. This automatically
manages the reusable memory buffer for the batch and allows the implementer to
write the raw event payload as a sequence of bytes. The function evts.Len returns the
maximum number of events allowed in a batch.

The choice of the format of the event payload is up to the plugin author, because the Plugin API allows both the encoding (in our example, for simplicity, we store the whole line as plain text in the payload) and the decoding of the data (as we will see in a moment). This permits you to create fields that you can use in rules. Choosing the correct format is essential because it has implications both for performance and for compatibility with other plugins (other authors may want to implement an extractor plugin that works with your events).

So far, you have seen the minimum set of methods required to implement a source plugin. However, the plugin would not really be useful at this point if we did not add a way to export fields to use in rule conditions and output.

Adding Field Extraction Capability

Plugins with field extraction capability can extract values from the event data and export fields that Falco can use. A plugin can have only event sourcing capability (described in the previous section), only field extraction capability, or both (like our example plugin). A plugin with field extraction capability will work on data sources provided by other plugins, while a plugin with both capabilities usually works only on its own data source. However, the mechanism is the same, regardless of the data source. The SDK lets you define the following methods, which apply in both cases:

- `Fields` to declare which fields the plugin is able to extract
- `Extract` to extract the value of a given field from the event data

Let's implement those methods in our example plugin. The first method, `Fields`, returns a slice of `sdk.FieldEntry`. Each entry contains the specification of a single field. The following code tells Falco that the plugin can extract a field called `shell.command` (this example adds just one field):

```
func (b *bashPlugin) Fields() []sdk.FieldEntry {
    return []sdk.FieldEntry{
        {Type: "string", Name: "shell.command", Display: "Shell command line",
         Desc: "The command line typed by user in the shell"},
    }
}
```

Now, to make the extraction work, we need to implement the `Extract` method, which provides the actual business logic to extract the field. The method receives as arguments an extraction request (which contains the identifier of the requested field) and a reader (to access the event payload). Implementing it is straightforward since this example has just one field and will simply return all the content of the event payload. In a real-world scenario, you would usually have more fields and specific logic to extract each of them:

```
func (m *bashPlugin) Extract(req sdk.ExtractRequest, evt sdk.EventReader) error {
    bb, err := io.ReadAll(evt.Reader())
    if err != nil {
        return err
    }

    switch req.FieldID() {
    case 0: // shell.command
        req.SetValue(string(bb))
        return nil
    default:
        return fmt.Errorf("unsupported field: %s", req.Field())
    }
}
```

With the field extraction capability in place, our example plugin is nearly ready. Let's see how to complete and use it.

Finalizing the Plugin

You're almost there. Next, you'll create an instance of the plugin and register its capabilities with the SDK. You can do that during the Go initialization phase by using the special init function (*https://oreil.ly/LDPaK*). (Do not confuse this with the Init method!) Since our example plugin has both source and extractor capabilities, we have to inform the SDK of both using the provided functions:

```
func init() {
    plugins.SetFactory(func() plugins.Plugin {
        p := &bashPlugin{}
        extractor.Register(p)
        source.Register(p)
        return p
    })
}

func main() {}
```

Note the empty main function. As you will see in a moment, the Go building system requires this to build the plugin correctly, but it will never call main, so you can always leave it empty.

The last step to make your code a real Go project is to initialize the Go module and download the dependencies:

```
$ go mod init example.com/my/plugin
$ go mod tidy
```

These commands create the *go.mod* and *go.sum* files, respectively. The code for your plugin is now ready. It's time to compile it so that you can use it with Falco!

Building a Plugin Written in Go

A plugin is a shared library (also called a *shared object*)—specifically, a compiled file—that exports a set of C symbols required by the plugin framework. (The SDK we used in the example hides those C symbols by using high-level interfaces, but they are still present underneath.)

The Go compiler has a specific command called cgo (*https://oreil.ly/sD0aW*) for creating Go packages that interface with C code. It allows you to compile your plugin and get a shared library file (a *.so* or *.dll* file). The command is pretty straightforward. From the same folder where the source code lives, run:

```
$ go build -buildmode=c-shared -o libmyplugin.so
```

This command creates *libmyplugin.so*, which you can use with Falco. (By convention, shared object files in Unix-like systems start with *lib* and have *.so* as their extension.) You learned about plugin configuration in Chapter 10, but the following section will give you some hints about using plugins while developing.

Using Plugins While Developing

By default, Falco looks for installed plugins at */usr/share/falco/plugins*. However, you can specify an absolute path in the configuration and place your plugin wherever you want. (That's convenient while developing, since you won't need to install the plugin in the default path.) We suggest building the plugin (using the command in the previous section) in the same folder you are using to develop it. Then, in the same folder, create a copy of *falco.yaml*, add your plugin configuration accordingly, and set the library_path option to the absolute path of your plugin. For example:

```
plugins:
  - name: bash
    library_path: /path/to/your/plugin/libmyplugin.so
    init_config: ""

load_plugins: [bash]
```

Now, before using your plugin, you need a rules file that matches the data source provided by the plugin. (Falco would load the plugin even without the rules file, but you wouldn't get any notifications.) You can create a rules file in the same folder—for instance, *myplugin_rules.yaml*—and add a rule like the following to it:

```
- rule: Cat in the shell
  desc: Match command lines starting with "cat".
  condition: shell.command startswith "cat "
  output: Cat in shell detected (command=%shell.command)
  priority: DEBUG
  source: bash
```

Once you have prepared both your customized *falco.yaml* and *myplugin_rules.yaml*, the very last step is to run Falco and pass those files in the respective options:

```
$ falco -c falco.yaml -r myplugin_rules.yaml
```

Done! This way of running a plugin in Falco is very convenient during development, since it does not require you to install any files or mess with your local Falco installation.

 If you built the plugin in our example, to trigger the rule, you can run:

```
$ bash
$ cat --version
$ exit
```

Conclusion

There are several ways of extending Falco. Writing a plugin is generally the best option, especially if you want Falco to work with a new data source to enable new use cases. The gRPC API may help you if you need to interface with outputs. On rare occasions, you may need to modify the Falco core and its components directly.

Whatever the case, you will need to read the documentation. You may sometimes need to study and understand advanced topics. Since Falco is open source and a collaborative project, you always have the opportunity to get in touch with its vibrant community. Sharing ideas and knowledge with others will help you find answers faster.

You may also discover that other people have your exact needs and are willing to help you improve or extend Falco. That would be a perfect opportunity to contribute to the Falco project. Everyone can contribute to Falco. Not only is it a rewarding experience, but contributing is a great help to the project and all of its users, including you. Want to know how? Read the next chapter!

CHAPTER 15

How to Contribute

Reaching this point in the book means you're on your way to mastering all aspects of Falco. This chapter will give you some advice on contributing to The Falco Project. Contributing means much more than just writing code (a common misconception)—in fact, there are many valuable ways to contribute. We'll explain where to start and how to satisfy the Falcosecurity organization's specific contribution requirements.

Contributing to open source software is a rewarding experience. Not only will you improve Falco, but you'll also meet people with similar interests, share feedback and ideas with others, and improve your own skills. If you are new to open source or want to learn more, we suggest taking a look at the Open Source Guides (*https://oreil.ly/ZBe39*).

What Does It Mean to Contribute to Falco?

Falco is a Cloud Native Computing Foundation (*https://www.cncf.io*) project. The CNCF serves as a vendor-neutral place for cloud native software. It empowers self-governing models for its hosted projects and helps sustain healthy open source communities. Falco is primarily driven by its community, which includes users, maintainers, and developers who curate and continuously improve it by:

- Sharing feedback to improve the design and existing features
- Testing Falco to discover issues
- Reporting bugs
- Writing project documentation
- Experimenting with new ideas
- Test-driving new features

- Proposing changes
- Writing code

And the list goes on. In summary, contributing means sharing knowledge and collaborating for the benefit of The Falco Project.

Where Should I Start?

You should start by joining the Falco community. You can do that by joining the Falco Slack channel (*https://oreil.ly/00Az6*) and introducing yourself. The community is very welcoming. We recommend subscribing to the official mailing list (*https://oreil.ly/R5CSB*). Community members, including maintainers, also get together in a weekly call, which everyone can join. You can find details about the weekly community call and other initiatives in the community GitHub repository (*https://oreil.ly/VMhp4*).

As a friendly reminder, the community is made up of human beings: be kind with them, and they will do the same with you. Everyone participating in the community must adhere to its Code of Conduct (*https://oreil.ly/GgbyC*), so make sure you read and understand it.

Contributing to Falcosecurity Projects

As you know by now, Falco and all its related projects are hosted under the Falcosecurity organization on GitHub (*https://oreil.ly/KNTDD*). Each project has its own public repository—you can even find a repository with the source code of the Falco website (*https://oreil.ly/47j3K*). If you don't have a GitHub account yet, you'll need to create one (*https://oreil.ly/F61GW*). We also advise you to take your time and get familiar with how GitHub works. You'll need a working knowledge of Git, particularly if you plan to contribute code.

The Falcosecurity organization has an automated support mechanism (or bot) to help you and make the contribution process easier. You will probably need a bit of time to get acquainted with it. If you need help, feel free to ask! An actual human from the community will be happy to help you.

Before preparing any contribution, make sure to check out the online contribution guidelines (*https://oreil.ly/yRema*), since they change from time to time. However, keep reading and we will explain the most important aspects.

Issues

GitHub issues (*https://oreil.ly/cOTct*) are the main way to interact with a project. Opening an issue to report a bug or propose an enhancement is one of the principal forms of contribution. Using issues correctly is also vital for the project, since most feedback comes from them.

Each Falcosecurity repository defines *kinds* of issues. The most common kinds are *Bug Report, Documentation Request, Failing Test,* and *Feature Request.* You select the kind when opening an issue. Depending on the kind you select, you will see an issue description along with a form for you to fill out. The form usually includes questions: for example, it might ask you to describe a bug, how to reproduce it, the Falco version that presents the bug, and so on. This information helps others understand your issue and work on it, so it's crucial to answer all of the questions to save everyone time and increase the chances of successful resolution.

Once an issue has been opened, a collaborative process starts. Any community members interested in the topic can participate, not just maintainers. Participating in this process is a welcome way to get involved.

The initial stage of this process is called *triaging.* It involves verifying and categorizing the information reported in the issue. For example, in the case of a bug, community members try to reproduce it and check if it appears in the manner described. In some cases, the process ends with someone correctly answering a question or simply pointing the reporter to resources that solve the problem. In other cases, someone volunteers to implement a requested feature or fix a bug and takes ownership of submitting a *pull request* (see the next section).

You can be involved at any stage of this process. As long as it is constructive, everyone can contribute.

Pull Requests

Pull requests (PRs) (*https://oreil.ly/bcerI*) are the only way to commit changes to a Falcosecurity project. When you want to submit a new feature or a fix, you have to fork the related repository (*https://oreil.ly/yfuIq*), create a branch in your fork, and add your commits. Once you're confident your change works as expected, you are ready to submit a PR. Similar to issues, PRs come with a predefined template (*https://oreil.ly/zqqJL*) to fill out. Be sure to read the instructions carefully. The template also includes some commands to help you interact with the automation.

After you open a PR, you will need to wait for a maintainer to review it. Maintainers have a lot of ongoing issues and PRs to look at, so be patient if they do not reply quickly! They might approve the PR directly or ask you to change something in your code. The review process is collaborative: maintainers and the PR author (and sometimes other users) share feedback and comments until the PR gets approved and merged. Any time you're in doubt, ask for support: the maintainers will explain how to proceed.

There are a few general guidelines to follow when making a PR:

- Each repository may have its own coding style and guidelines; make sure you read and understand them.

- Avoid proposing too many code changes in a single PR; submitting several smaller, self-contained PRs usually works better.

- Maintainers highly recommend using the Conventional Commits style (*https://oreil.ly/BB160*) in your Git commit messages.

- You must sign off on all of your Git commits, and your PR must not include merge commits (which we'll discuss in a moment).

The following subsections explain the main requirements you must satisfy when preparing your code using Git.

Git conflict resolution and linear history

Sometimes you may need to synchronize with the upstream (remote) branch when working on your PR. If the remote branch has diverged from your local one, conflicts might arise. Git allows you to synchronize and resolve conflicts by *merging* or *rebasing*. Both methods solve the same problem, but they produce different outcomes.

Merging happens when the histories of the local and remote branches have diverged, and you use the `git merge` command or the `git pull` command to reconcile nonlinear histories. However, merging has the drawback of not leaving the repository history clean, making it harder to navigate with commands like `git bisect` or `git log`. For these reasons, the Falcosecurity organization does not allow merging in its projects.

In contrast, *rebasing* moves your commits, placing them on top of the history of the other branch (instead of introducing a merge commit). That ensures the Git history is always linear. When developing your PR, you must always use rebasing to synchronize with the upstream or resolve conflicts with the main branch. The following command works in both cases (replace *<branch>* with the name of the remote branch):

```
$ git fetch origin
$ git rebase -i origin/<branch>
```

This command also removes merge commits if you have accidentally introduced them. You can use its shortened version, `git pull --rebase`, when you only need to pull changes from your remote branch (for example, when working with collaborators on the same branch).

To reiterate: the Falcosecurity organization enforces a linear history and does not allow merge commits for any projects. If your PR has a merge commit, the automation will block the PR and maintainers will not be able to merge it until you fix the issue. Always use rebasing, or your changes will not be accepted.

The Developer Certificate of Origin

In 2004, the Linux Foundation (the parent organization of the CNCF) introduced the Developer Certificate of Origin (DCO) (*https://oreil.ly/Qttlz*), a lightweight way for contributors to state that they have written (or have the right to submit) a piece of code. Projects that enforce the DCO require contributors to sign off on their commits, indicating that they agree to the DCO's terms for that single contribution. The Git CLI has an embedded sign-off functionality that you can use via the `-s` option (*https://oreil.ly/5VcWl*) or by manually adding the following line to the commit message:

```
Signed-off-by: Full Name <example@example.net>
```

The line must follow this format and include your name and email address.

As part of the CNCF, Falco and all its related projects require the DCO. The Falco-security organization implements an automation mechanism to check the DCO on PRs. When it is missing in a commit, the automation blocks the PR. So, don't forget to sign off on every single commit; otherwise, maintainers cannot accept your contributions.

If you submit a PR and the DCO check fails because you missed signing off on one or more commits, don't worry. You can adjust it. If you just need to amend the last commit, use:

```
$ git commit --amend --signoff
$ git push --force-with-lease
```

If you need to fix all the commits in your PR, use:

```
$ git rebase --signoff origin
$ git push --force-with-lease
```

Conclusion

Congratulations, you've reached the end of the book! It's been a long journey that covered architecture, syntax, real-world usage, customization, code development, and many more interesting topics. We sincerely hope you've enjoyed reading it and, more importantly, that the content is valuable to you, whether you came to this book as a beginner or an advanced user.

For us, this is a bittersweet moment. While we are sad to say goodbye, we're grateful we had a chance to go through this journey with you, and we are proud to contribute to making your software a little more secure.

You are now ready to start another incredible adventure. As Falco maintainers, we welcome you to the project and hope to meet you in one of the community forums.

Index

About the Authors

Loris Degioanni is the CTO and founder of Sysdig. He's also the creator of sysdig, the popular open source troubleshooting tool, as well as the CNCF runtime security tool Falco. Loris was one of the original contributors to Wireshark, the open source network analyzer. He holds a PhD in computer engineering from Politecnico di Torino and lives in Davis, California.

Leonardo Grasso is an open source software engineer at Sysdig and a core maintainer of The Falco Project. He has a strong passion for software design and long professional experience in the R&D field. Leonardo loves contributing to open source projects from his home in Italy and enjoys building tools other engineers would like to use.

Colophon

The animal on the cover of *Practical Cloud Native Security with Falco* is a red-necked falcon (*Falco chicquera*).

Red-necked falcons are medium-size, long-winged birds of prey occurring in two distinct populations—one in Africa, the other in India—that genetic studies suggest have been separate for nearly one million years. As such, they are often treated as different species, with the African "subspecies" *Falco chicquera ruficollis* given the species name *Falco ruficollis*.

In both India and Africa, these falcons are often found in open habitats, though in Africa they may also inhabit riverine forests. They typically hunt in pairs, sometimes utilizing a coordinated technique in which one falcon flushes up small birds from below and the other seizes the prey from above. The prowess to which this attests is perhaps one reason they were once a favorite among Indian falconers.

The Indian variant of red-necked falcons has been categorized by IUCN as *near threatened* due to declining population. The African variant is listed as of *least concern*. Many of the animals on O'Reilly covers are endangered; all of them are important to the world.

The cover illustration is by Karen Montgomery, based on an antique line engraving from Wood's *Animate Creation*. The cover fonts are Gilroy Semibold and Guardian Sans. The text font is Adobe Minion Pro; the heading font is Adobe Myriad Condensed; and the code font is Dalton Maag's Ubuntu Mono.

Lightning Source UK Ltd.
Milton Keynes UK
UKHW051010230822
407646UK00009B/31

9 781098 118570